SURVIVING
the PRODIGALS
in your LIFE

Stories of Courage and Hope

WOODROW KROLL

BACK TO THE BIBLE
Publishing

SURVIVING THE PRODIGALS IN YOUR LIFE
by Woodrow Kroll

All Scripture quotations, unless otherwise indicated, are taken from the HOLY BIBLE: NEW INTERNATIONAL VERSION®, copyright 1973, 1978, 1984 by The International Bible Society. Used by permission of Zondervan Publishing House. All rights reserved.

BACK TO THE BIBLE PUBLISHING
P. O. Box 82808
Lincoln, Nebraska 68501

Editor: Allen Bean
Proofreaders: Susan Hertzler, Kim Johnson
Cover and interior design: Laura Poe
Art direction: Kim Johnson

Additional copies of this book are available from Back to the Bible Publishing. You may order by calling 1-800-759-2425 or through our Web site at www.resources.backtothebible.org.

1 2 3 4 5 6 7 8 9 10 – 06 05 04 03 02 01

ISBN 0-8474-1280-6

Printed in the USA

Table of Contents

PREFACE

Americans were mesmerized. Fifty-one million of them. They couldn't get enough. It swept the country, not to mention the TV ratings, by storm. CBS finally had a winner—a big winner. It was the king of reality TV. A program called *Survivor*.

The program idea was simple enough. Drop 16 people off on the remote island of Sabah, Malaysia, make them fend for themselves under adverse, sometimes impossible, circumstances, and film their every move, day and night. Pit one team against another, and then one player against another, and bring out the best, or worst, in all of them. All they had to do was outwit, outplay and outlast everyone else. People were glued to their television sets for weeks.

Survivor. There's something magical, almost mystical, about the word. The whole idea of being a survivor appeals to people. We all want to be survivors. Some survive the death of a spouse; others survive the breakup of a marriage. A survivor is one who hangs in there and continues to function after facing extreme difficulty.

Do you know what Kate Conolly, Khalil Saad, Luigi Finote, Anna Saljilsvik and Baron von Drachstedt have in common? They are all survivors.

When 2224 people set sail on the Titanic, all of them expected to be survivors. But when the unsinkable ship hit that iceberg on April 14, 1912, there were only 712 survivors. These people were among them.

There were no survivors when the French Concorde crashed on takeoff July 25, 2000, from a Paris airport. There were, however, 113 casualties. Survivors are special people. They are like Jesse Knowles, who survived the Bataan death march. Or Mike Connelly, Paul Heath and Rob Roddy, who survived the Oklahoma City bombing. They beat the odds. They encountered incredibly disturbing circumstances and came through them alive.

This book is about being a survivor. A special kind of survivor. It's about surviving the prodigals in your life.

My purpose in writing *Surviving the Prodigals in Your Life* was threefold. First, like many of you, I have been enamored with Jesus' parable of the prodigal son since the first time I read it. There are so many nuances to this story, so much buried treasure. I wanted to exegete the passage and find some of it. This parable deserves careful, biblical, expository examination. But I didn't want to make a story sound like a Bible commentary. So in the pages that follow, you will find an expository parable, an exegetical story, directly from the lips of the Master.

Second, there is so much to learn here about how to turn your life around if you are a prodigal. There is hope that you can go home again. The younger son in Jesus' story is the most instructive person in the Bible, perhaps in the whole of history, as to how a prodigal can come to himself and find his or her way home. It's a story of courage and hope. And there is no more instructive piece in ancient or modern literature on how to receive a runaway prodigal back again. Jesus presents an alternative to letting our hurt feelings drive our actions when a prodigal wants to come home.

Finally, it appears that Jesus' purpose in telling the parable was to address the relationship of the father to both his sons, not just one. This made being a survivor doubly difficult for the father. He had two prodigals to deal with, not just one. The first prodigal left home; the second one didn't.

This story needs to be understood in the context in which Jesus told it. Here we will focus on surviving every prodigal in your life, even the ones who don't see themselves as prodigals.

If you are on the run from God, this book is for you. If you have a son or daughter who is away from the Lord, this book is for you. If you are sandwiched between two prodigals, this book is especially for you. If others find you a bit crabby toward those prodigals in your life, this book is also for you. This is the story of the prodigal sons and the father who loved them both. It is arguably the most tender and most tragic parable in the Bible.

As you read, look for yourself. Let Jesus touch your heart and teach you how to handle the prodigals in your life, and survive. Let Him show you how you can go home again if you have wandered away from your family, and survive. Let Him open your eyes to the potential that even though you have not been unfaithful to the family or to your church, you may be the biggest prodigal of all. Be open to anything, and discover who you are in this story.

Let God use this book to change your attitudes. Let Him use it to change your expectations. Let Him use it to change your life.

Woodrow Kroll—Lincoln, Nebraska

INTRODUCTION

Words are the tools of language. They are to verbal communication what paint and brush are to a canvas. Say a word, speak an image or an idea. Brush a stroke and do the same thing.

Take the word *family*, for example. That word paints a broad stroke. You may conjure up an image of beautiful harmony, painted with complementary hues of green and yellow. Or *family* to you may paint a disharmony so painful it defies description. Sometimes the strokes of a brush give the impression of harmony, when just beneath the surface lies a hideous mixture of paint that is ugly and shocking. Frequently that's true with families as well.

Everybody loves a good story, and a good storyteller. While we think of Jesus as Savior, Messiah and Lord, He was also a great storyteller. Many of His stories were parables, including His best story—a story about a family. It was the parable of the prodigal son. Actually, it's a story about a father and his two sons. Long before anyone ever heard of a dysfunctional family, Jesus was telling stories about one.

Three Stories; One Truth

Recorded in Luke 15 are three strikingly similar stories of Jesus, including the one about the dysfunctional family. Each story reflects the tragedy of loss, the grief of the loser, and the joy of recovery.

The first of Jesus' stories depicts the pastoral life; the second the peasant life; the third the parental life. The first story is set outdoors—in the wilderness. The second is a bit more domesticated—indoors but in a peasant woman's home with a dirt floor. The third is the most magnificent of all. It occurs in the home of a wealthy landowner.

If you've ever wondered why Jesus told three stories and in this order—lost sheep, lost coin, lost son—the answer is simple. It's not a question of value—a son is more valuable than a coin, a coin more valuable than a sheep. It's a question of proportion.

In Jesus' first story a shepherd had 100 sheep in the wilderness. One of those sheep quietly and unobtrusively nibbled itself farther and farther from the flock until it nibbled itself lost. The shepherd left the 99 sheep with other shepherds and went out to seek the one.

Why? Because one sheep in 100 was important to the shepherd.

In the second story a woman had 10 coins. She dropped one of them and it rolled out of sight, probably into some dark crack in her dirt floor. The woman swept the house from stem to stern to find the lost coin. Why? Because one coin in 10 was important to the peasant woman.

In the third story a father had two sons. One of them wandered away from the life of the family, and the father longingly awaited his return. Why? Because one son in two was important to the father.

God Is Interested in the Individual

Do you see the proportion in these stories? One in 100. One in 10. One in two. By the time Jesus got to His story about the dysfunctional family, He had already primed our appreciation that God is interested in the individual. His tender heart is touched with you and me as people.

God loves people, all people, individual people. As Ralph Waldo Emerson said, "Souls are not saved in bundles." God draws us to Himself and saves us one at a time. You can never fully appreciate these stories until you appreciate how marvelously sympathetic the heart of the Storyteller is.

For the most part our lives are lived in groups. We are members of families, cities, nations, races, etc. The admiral orders, "All hands on deck." The sergeant barks, "Company dismissed." The professor begins his lecture saying, "Class, come to order." When the judge enters, the courtroom rings with, "All rise." We live in groups. Our lives are lived as collective nouns.

Even when we are individualized, frequently we are depersonalized. We have Social Security numbers, credit card numbers, telephone numbers. All of these are individual, but very impersonal. Can you get any more impersonal than accessing your ATM by punching in your personal identification number?

But God is very different. He knows the number of hairs on your head. He knows your name. He has given you fingerprints, a DNA code and a voiceprint that no one else in the whole world has. He knows all there is to know about you. He knows what your relationship is with His Son, Jesus Christ. God knows you individually and He cares for you personally.

Why a Family Parable?

The third of Jesus' parables in Luke 15 is a story about a family caught in a web of impersonal relationships with each other. It's the story of the nuclear family, the American family, the church family. It's the story of a family painted in pastels on the surface but with deep and angry colors just beneath.

This is a parable of strained relationships, of pent-up emotions and of two events that caused those emotions to erupt like a volcano. It's a family portrait. Look at the faces of the father and his sons. See the face of the younger son—strained, unhappy, masking his true feelings for his father. See the face of the older brother—smug, satisfied and self-righteous. See the face of the father—smiling, thankful, hopeful that real harmony will grace their family portrait.

Keep this portrait on the sticky side of your mind as you read this book. You'll understand the parable of the prodigal son better if you view it through the skillful strokes of the divine Artist. He painted a masterpiece about relationships, about attitudes, about people just like you and me. Occasionally you may see yourself in the strokes of the Master.

Let's examine Jesus' portrait of the younger son, then the older brother, and finally the father. He's the man in the middle, the one who is doing his best to survive the prodigals in his life. Take a closer look at the canvas.

Let's examine Jesus' portrait of the younger son, then the older brother, and finally the father. He's the man in the middle, the one who is doing his best to survive the prodigals in his life. Take a closer look at the canvas.

HURTING PARENTS

Paul and Lucy Lufkin

"My life has been blessed by God," says Lucy Lufkin. "I have a godly husband, four children I dearly love, and a fulfilling ministry as a pastor's wife. Our oldest daughter, Stephanie, is now married. Just a few years ago my husband and I were giving thanks to God and trying hard not to pat ourselves on the back for the great job we did in raising our kids. We had heard the usual stories of the teen troubles people have, but, for the most part, we were spared those problems with our family."

The Lufkins do have good kids. They raised them with definite limits and loving discipline. When correction was needed Paul or Lucy would sit down with them, review what they did wrong and why it was wrong. They would then administer measured discipline, review again why the punishment was given, pray with their kids, and then reassure them that they loved them.

Life was good. Their home was the perfect picture of domestic tranquillity. It was like watching reruns of *Ozzie and Harriet*. They were going to make it.

And then it happened.

The Loss of Innocence

The tranquillity in the Lufkin home was smashed the summer after their second daughter, Amy, graduated from high school. "Amy had not dated much during school, but now she was making up for lost time," Paul said with a smile. "Initially we were happy that she finally had a social life. But suddenly she was going through boyfriends like mosquitoes through a broken screen." Paul's smile waned. The Lufkins could have lived with that, but as parents they began to wonder what she was doing on her frequent dates. All parents do. But Amy had never given them any cause to worry before; why were they so apprehensive now?

11

It wasn't long, however, until their worst suspicions were confirmed. Amy had been raised with Christian values. She knew the difference between right and wrong. The moral standards of the Bible had always been lived out before her and inculcated in her. But she threw them to the wind on her dates with these boys. Like the boy in the prodigal son story, she craved the freedom to make her own decisions, to live her life as she wanted. She saw that as something that had eluded her in a loving home.

Lucy remembers, "Just a few days before Christmas four years ago, she informed us she was not planning to be home over the holidays. When we questioned her, Amy insisted she preferred to spend Christmas with a guy she was dating and his family in another city." Paul and Lucy knew that spelled trouble, so they told her that wasn't a good idea and she should plan on spending Christmas with her family. Well, there was a mega-explosion, measuring near the double digits on the Richter Scale. She blew up and summarily walked out the door. Shortly afterward Amy moved out of the Lufkin house and in with her boyfriend.

She was gone. Their little girl had chosen to live with a stranger rather than live with her family. The Lufkins tried to console themselves that at least they knew where she was and that she would be okay, but they were just fooling themselves.

Serious Abuse

Some time later Paul and Lucy became aware that Amy's boyfriend was abusive to her. He was using her and she couldn't see it. The abuse was on every level and getting more serious. Once it was so threatening that she called her dad and mom for help. They drove immediately to the apartment where Amy and her boyfriend were living, picked her up and took her to the police station. Imagine. The pastor and his wife at the police station with their daughter. How humiliating.

Because there were no bruises, the police couldn't do anything except escort her back to the apartment to gather her things and go home with the Lufkins. That's when the strangest thing happened. The guy was at home by the time the police and Lufkins arrived with Amy. He was angry but controlled in front of the police. He began to peel away the armor that Amy had built up against him.

He had this strange emotional hold over her. It wasn't long before he talked her out of leaving him. Again she had chosen a stranger over her parents. The hands of the police were tied. "We left brokenhearted," Lucy said, "afraid that the only way she would get out of that relationship would be in a body bag." That was a real possibility.

Amy lived with Rick for 20 months, until one day she finally decided she had enough. There would be no more lies, no more abuse, no more tears. She knew she had made a big mistake in moving in with him, and Paul and Lucy's prodigal daughter wanted to come home. When she called, they were delighted, almost speechless. But they soon learned that while she was coming home, it wasn't necessarily out of remorse for what she had done to them. Amy ran up a considerable credit card debt and Dad and Mom were the bank. They could accept that, however; it was just good to have their prodigal home again.

Home Again

With Amy back home, Lucy thought their problems were now behind them. Was she ever wrong. Amy's been home for more than two years now and life has been tough for her, and for the Lufkins. Those 20 months living a sinful lifestyle left Amy spiritually and emotionally unstable. She has had difficulty adjusting to life back home, as well as to her brothers, who are both younger than she.

Amy's home behavior has its ups and downs. When the downs hit, they really hit. Just this past December she threatened to commit suicide. Paul and Lucy intervened and sought help for her. She spent three days in the county crisis center. It was quite an ordeal for the whole family.

As Christian parents Paul and Lucy wondered, *How can this be happening to us? We always tried to do the right things for our kids. We trained them as they should go. What happened? What went wrong?* There were no immediate answers. In fact, there were no answers at all.

At least, they mused, *we did all right with three out of four.* But just as things started leveling out with Amy, things started happening with their boys. Some prodigals leave home; others do not.

More Prodigals

Jimmy is now 18; Jack is 20. Jimmy has been in trouble with the law before. Nothing too serious; but when the pastor's kid is in trouble, it's a big thing. He suffers from depression and is often uncommunicative. During his later teen years he has wanted nothing to do with Jesus or Christianity. At times, he has wanted nothing to do with his dad or mom, or even with his brother. He went to church with the family, but only because he had to. He never sang any of the hymns or praise choruses. He would just stare off into space to signal that he wasn't happy to be there.

Boys will be boys, and occasionally Jimmy would fight with his older brother. Sometimes he would even fight with Amy. He had trouble controlling his temper. Often he would turn away from Jack or Amy and slam his fist into the wall. Everybody knew that's what he wanted to do to them, but didn't dare.

One Sunday morning a real brouhaha developed. Lucy remembers, "My husband and I weren't home at the time, but the boys got into a real fight. Tempers flared, fists flew, and I came home to find a smashed guitar in our driveway. I didn't know what happened, but our van was missing. What was even more devastating, I discovered one of my husband's guns was also missing."

Jack had smashed Jimmy's guitar in anger during a fight. Jimmy threatened Jack with the gun, and it would have gotten even uglier had not Amy stepped in, grabbed the gun and then took Jack for a ride to cool off. What was happening to the Lufkin home? They just couldn't understand. It wasn't supposed to be like this, not for a Christian family, not for the pastor's family.

Eventually things quieted down. They took Jimmy to the doctor for his anger and depression. He is now on medication. He also had to go through a diversion program for the trouble he got into, including 30 hours of community service as a part of his diversion.

One of their prodigals left home and came back. The other never left home but caused equal havoc.

Progress Report

So how are our prodigals doing now? Paul says, "I wish I could tell you there has been a dramatic turnaround and that we have no more worries. There has been a dramatic turnaround, but our lives will never be the same."

Jimmy now goes to church regularly on Sunday evenings and sporadically on Sunday mornings. Even better news is that now he fully participates in the service. He sings the hymns. He bows his head during prayer (that never happened before). He has begun to take Communion again. There's light at the end of the tunnel, and it's not an oncoming train. It's the light of real hope.

"Wednesday of last week was a very busy day," notes Lucy. "Supper was catch-as-catch-can. Thank God for microwaves. Everybody just warmed up some leftovers and helped themselves. It's not usually like that, but yesterday was just one of those days. As I was puttering around the kitchen, I saw Jimmy zap some food in the microwave and go over to the table to eat. I watched in silent joy as I saw him bow his head and thank God for His goodness. And it wasn't just one of those 'headache prayers' where you do a quick up-and-down and rub your brow a bit. It was a bona fide, genuine, sincere prayer. Last year at this time Jimmy wouldn't even bow his head or close his eyes during prayer. He's come so far."

When Lucy picked up Amy after work the other day, she had to wait about 15 minutes for her to arrive at the minivan. "She has always been the poky one, but I wondered what could be taking her so long? Turns out she had been talking to a coworker who has been dealing with two years of sexual abuse in his past. She was encouraging him to get back to church and establish a relationship with the Lord. That about blew my mind. My troubled Amy, a counselor? God is so good."

By the way, Amy's new boyfriend and her best friend each talked with Paul separately this past Sunday about taking membership classes to join the church. Paul speculates, "I think that has been Amy's influence on them both."

Lessons for Parents of Prodigals

Have Paul and Lucy, as parents, learned anything from the "kid wars" they've been through? You bet. Here are some things God has impressed on them. You'll find many of these true for you as well.

First, they aren't all the way home yet. Prodigal stories only have relative degrees of happy endings. It's true things are much better at home for the Lufkins than they have been for years, but it will not be until they are finally home—to their heavenly home—that they can take a breather. Raising kids is a lifelong task, and often a mixed blessing. "We're glad to be where we are as a family," Lucy reminds us, "but we haven't arrived yet. There could be more trouble in the future, and if there is, we'll face it holding the Lord's hand as we have in the past."

Second, every sign of improvement in their children's interpersonal relationships is a sign of victory for the Lufkins. When you have prodigals in your family, all victories, even the little ones, are cause for celebration.

Paul shared this example. "All three of the kids still at home went willingly with us to Wichita, Kansas, last fall for a Ligonier Ministries conference. We wanted them to go, but were surprised when they agreed. And here's the best thing. After the conference was over, our Jimmy stood in line for the longest time just to speak to R. C. Sproul and thank him for a video series he had seen in Sunday school. Was I ever amazed. God is so good."

Third, Lucy says, "My experience with my prodigal children has changed my life in ways I could never have dreamed. I was also a PK and pretty much toed the line all my life. I remember being almost envious of the testimonies I heard from people who were saved from all kinds of sins. Now I see in my kids, hopefully, the makings of great testimonies. And I also have seen the travail that gives birth to these testimonies. My envy was misplaced! I wouldn't wish this process on anyone, but I'm sure glad that God does indeed work all things together for good to those who love Him, to the called according to His purpose."

Finally, Lucy especially has been tenderly touched by the Savior's lament over Jerusalem. He would have gathered His people as a mother hen gathers her chicks, yet they would have none of it. "I can identify with the longing and sorrow that comes when you see someone you love choose a path that leads them away from you. Nobody can break your heart like your children," she said.

Lucy continues, "I wouldn't be truthful if I didn't tell you I have been hurt deeply in all of this. I did what I thought was right as a parent. I raised my kids in a Christian environment. I leaned heavily on verses like Proverbs 22:6, 'Train up a child in the way he should go, and when he is old he will not depart from it.' Well, maybe I haven't given that verse a full lifetime to work."

Yet both Paul and Lucy believe God can change people—even their children—in His own time. They take comfort in the stories of good Christian people who followed similar self-destructive paths before finally coming to rest in their Savior. Each story proves to them that there is hope, real hope for prodigals and their parents.

After months and months of telling their kids "I love you" and receiving only silent stares in return, Paul and Lucy are finally hearing them respond. Sometimes they even say it first. Lucy asks, "Is there anything better than a prodigal son or daughter telling you, 'I love you, Mom'? I can't think of a thing! God is so good."

Part One

THE RUNAWAY KID

Why Kids Run Away From Home and Why They Come Back

Chapter 1

HOW DEEP THE HURT

"Drop dead!"

Nobody likes to hear them. They're words that cut us deeply. "Drop dead!" Sometimes the wound is deepest when these words take feet. That usually happens when someone is so self-absorbed they don't care about anyone else.

A British newspaper carried an item about two famous men—one a painter, the other a writer. James McNeill Whistler and Oscar Wilde were seen at Brighton talking about themselves. Whistler clipped the article and sent it to his friend with this comment: "I wish these reporters would be more accurate. If you remember, Oscar, we were talking about me." Wilde responded, "It is true, Jimmie, we were talking about you, but I was thinking of myself."

The Demanding Son

This prodigal in Jesus' story may not have been that conceited, but he was self-absorbed. Like a lot of us, he was convinced that if he had never been born, people would want to know why.

This young man was not a bad boy. Jesus didn't say he was. But he was tarnished with selfishness. He had a "The world owes me" attitude toward life. He also had a "You don't understand what's best for me" attitude toward his father. Not uncommon attitudes, even in the 21st century.

The younger son spoke freely and disrespectfully to his father in a demanding way. It's not so much what he said as what he didn't say. There were no "please and thank yous" in his demand. "Father, give me my share of the estate" (Luke 15:12). He was very direct, but not very gracious.

Look at the canvas. Peer into his face. See the contempt. Listen to the tone of his voice—"Give me." This was not a request; it was a demand. The tense of the verb in the original language suggests it was more of an ultimatum. The prodigal did not plead with his father. He demanded—"Give me."

You fathers may be saying to yourself, "If my son ever came to me with such a demand, I know what I'd give him." That's human nature. But the father in Jesus' story responded differently. That's what's so amazing about this parable—the graciousness of the father in the face of his son's ungracious attitude.

If you're like I am, you've found that one of the hardest things about parenting is not acting like a parent. Throughout this story the father responded more like our Heavenly Father does to us than we do to our children. Dads, the strokes that Jesus painted in this portrait of the father are strokes God wants to paint in our lives.

Jesus said, "So he divided his property between them" (v. 12). The father acquiesced to his son's demands by dividing the inheritance between his sons. The older boy said nothing. He did not shake his fist in the father's face and demand his inheritance. But don't miss this: The father divided the inheritance between both sons. He did not just give the younger son what he demanded; he gave the older son what he didn't demand.

Do you think he was right in what he did? Did Jesus paint a portrait of a weak father, one who simply caved in to the demands of his son? I don't think so. Just as there are some sheep prone to wander, there are some sons similarly prone. I think this was not the first time the prodigal demanded something of his father. The story line fits nicely the "last straw" scenario.

It's possible the younger son had been a boil on his father's back for years—always whining, always complaining. Likely he grumbled about having to work in the field. He probably feigned a stomachache when it was time to go to the barn. Maybe his father's expectations were a long-standing irritation to him. This was not the first time he insulted his father, but it would be his last.

Sometimes, Dad and Mom, you have instilled your values in your children; you have disciplined and chastened them in love; still they act selfishly. Sometimes you just have to commit your children to God's woodshed. You don't love them any less. Quite the contrary. You love them enough to commit them to God's care.

The Law of Inheritance

Let's digress from Jesus' story a moment. We'll better understand why the boy's demand was so important to the parable if we remember the law of inheritance in the Bible.

Question: In the Ancient Near East, was an inheritance awarded at death through the vehicle of a will? Did the younger son have the right to demand his portion of the inheritance? What's your answer?

Westerners frequently don't understand what all the fuss is about in the Middle East. Why do the Jews and Arabs seem to be feuding all the time? What do the Palestinians want? Why did Israel rush to capture the West Bank during the famous 1967 June War? And why does it seem to be in the news daily?

All these questions, indeed the whole Palestinian issue, are wrapped up in the law of inheritance. Historically, a fundamental principle of Hebrew society has been that real property always belonged to the family, not to the individual. Land was the possession of families, not members of families. It was passed from generation to generation within the family.

This concept originated when God awarded the Promised Land to Israel. The Mosaic Law's elaborate system of inheritance directed that, when a man died, his family land would be passed to his male heirs. If the man had no sons, the inheritance went to his daughters; if no daughters, to his brothers, etc. (Num. 27:8-11; Ruth 3:12-13). Land always stayed within the family.

When the State of Israel was founded in 1947, land that belonged to Arab families for hundreds of years was taken to create a homeland for the Jewish people. In 1967 the West Bank was added to Israel's territory. Again Palestinians were displaced and took up residence in Arab enclaves adjacent to the newly configured State of Israel.

The Jews lay claim to the land through the promises of God. The Palestinians lay claim to it through centuries of occupation. Hence, the Middle East conflict is about the right of a homeland.

Inheritance is inextricably tied to land, and land is the link to family history. No land, no history. No land, no identity. Take away inheritance, and you impact posterity. Take away land, and you impact ancestry.

The father in Jesus' story had the right to give gifts to his sons whenever he wanted, but generally such gifts would not be real estate. Only on rare occasions would a father give a parcel of land to his son (Gen. 25:6).

While fathers were discouraged from giving the inheritance of land to their sons before they died, it was their prerogative. That was acceptable. What was not acceptable was for the selfish son to ask for his inheritance before his father died.

How Deep the Hurt

The prodigal son was greedy, arrogant and unthankful. Most of all, he was just plain selfish. His "Give me" demand was out of line. Still, the gentle father divided the family inheritance between his sons, the older receiving the double portion by law.

That was no little feat, for the father had to sell a portion of land to relatives and convert it to cash. Imagine the stir this would have caused in town. Such transactions are never done quietly. Talk around town must have sizzled. What was happening in this family? Imagine the innuendoes and half-truths. Imagine the father's protracted agony while converting his holdings into liquid assets.

But an even greater insult in the prodigal's demand can be read between the lines. Inheritance was divided at the father's death, but the selfish prodigal demanded it while the father was living. This was tantamount to saying to the father, "Drop dead, so I can have my share of the family estate now."

Clearly the younger son valued his family inheritance more than he did his family. Selfishness does that. It tarnishes everything it touches. The prodigal prized property more than he prized people. When that is true for any of us, we are heading for God's woodshed.

There's quite a contrast here between the son's lust for the father's possessions and the father's love for the son. The father was willing to give up those possessions in one last attempt to salvage his son. That's how desperate things had become in this troubled home. The son, on the other hand, wasn't willing to give up anything.

The prodigal son was afflicted with a deadly disease—hardening of the attitudes. He cared little how his actions affected the family.

He was self-absorbed. He cared only for himself. He was determined to do what was best for himself regardless of the consequences to others.

Your Time Is Coming

Have you been there yet as a parent? If not, hold on; your time is coming. Few parents escape periodic bouts with prodigalism.

You love your son or daughter, you try to do what's right for them, you discipline them, you instill your values in them—and they just don't get it. They say you are oppressive and overbearing, inhibiting their freedom. There are constant shouting matches in your home. Frequent clashes of the will erupt. Demands lead to ultimatums. What should you do?

Begin by checking your *priorities*. What is really important to you? Is what your son or daughter demands so outrageous that you are willing to give them up rather than give it up? What's really important to you—your land or your son?

Maybe your son or daughter wants to stay out an extra hour or two on the weekends. Maybe they are demanding extra driving privileges. They want to take the car to school a few more days a week. Are these demands so significant that they're worth losing your children? Begin by checking your priorities. That's not a sign of weakness; that's a sign of wisdom.

Second, check the *possibilities*. The prodigal son demanded his portion of the inheritance. His demand was wrong, but was his claim legitimate? If your son or daughter demands one more hour on Saturday night, is one more hour unreasonable? Is their demand legitimate? Check the possibilities. Maybe you do owe them an extra hour, or an extra day of driving to school. Maybe their demand isn't so unreasonable after all. It's hard for moms or dads to see their kids as mature enough to handle anything, but maybe we just see them as our little children and don't recognize that they have grown up. Check the possibilities.

Then check their *patterns*. Have they consistently kept the rules you established for them? If their school night curfew is 11:00 p.m. and they want to stay out past midnight on weekends, have they earned the right by respecting your 11:00 p.m. curfew regularly? What are their patterns? Perhaps we do owe them more.

How faithful have they been in doing those little jobs around the house that are their dues for being a part of the family? If their patterns prove they're not just being selfish, maybe you should reconsider your position. Perhaps you're not giving in to their demands; rather you're rising to their level of proven trust.

Let Them Go

My daughter was in her sophomore year at college. One night she called home with the news that she had decided to get an apartment with two other dorm girls. They all thought it would be cheaper. As a typical father my initial response was a non-negotiable no. When I found out that my daughter was the only one of this trio with a job, my parental prohibition made all the more sense.

That night, after several discussions with my wife in which she pointed out the similarity between Jesus' parable and our situation, we agreed that if the girls set certain standards at the apartment, they could have one. The standards had to be tough and they had to be strictly observed. In a phone call the next morning, my daughter's sobs turned to tears of joy.

My daughter was not a prodigal; not at all. She was not acting selfishly like the prodigal. I had every reason to trust her. I still would have preferred she remain in the dorm, but there were lessons for her to learn that could not be mastered in dorm life. I acceded to her desires.

The father in Jesus' family portrait did not believe dividing the inheritance was the best thing for his selfish son, but there had to be lessons learned that could not be acquired at home. The father was right.

Sometimes you just have to let them go. That's when parents draw comfort from verses like Proverbs 22:6. That's when we increase our prayers for them and commit them to God.

Are you faced with a "Give me" situation with one of your children? Assess to what degree their demand is unreasonable. Is your child being selfish? Is this only natural or are they being tarnished by their selfishness? Weigh the potential harm of acceding to their demand as opposed to the harm of losing your child. Seek the counsel of your pastor or other mature Christian.

Being a parent is tough enough without having to deal with selfish children; but if you're faced with a selfish demand, begin by judging the reasonableness of the demand itself. Who knows, you may find yourself sympathizing with the prodigal's father. Do the right thing!

Chapter 2

WHY KIDS RUN AWAY FROM HOME

"I don't love you anymore!"

Every day 1.3 million runaway and homeless kids live on the streets of America.[1] It is estimated that in Seattle, Washington, 800 young people are on the streets on any given night.[2] That's tragic, but that's 21st–century America.

Ron and Marie were a high–profile family in their church. They were popular, leaders in so many things. Their life was typical of many Christians today. They taught Bible study groups, sponsored events in their home, and held offices in the church.

They loved their daughter Betsy. She was a young teen with a bright future. People would often comment to Marie, "You and Betsy look so much alike. You have a great relationship as mother and daughter." And it was true. Everything appeared to be running along smoothly in their lives.

But in junior high Betsy began to withdraw from her family. She effectively shut her mom and dad out of her life. She spent a lot of time in her room, on the phone, hanging out or just goofing off. She preferred a life of solitude to family life. Ron and Marie were puzzled at Betsy's behavior, but not worried.

Then one night Ron and Marie were out with some friends. They were gone for hours. When they returned they received the shock of their lives. Betsy had thrown a party in their absence. She invited some friends from school and several of them brought alcohol along. Things got a little out of hand.

When Ron and Marie broke up the party and confronted Betsy, she exploded. "I hate you. Leave me alone. I don't love you anymore!" This was her parents' first clue that Betsy was on the edge of becoming a prodigal daughter.

In the months that followed, the relationship between Betsy and her parents went from bad to worse. She began running with the wrong kids at school. Ron and Marie suspected their daughter was doing drugs, getting drunk and sexually active with the guys she dated.

One night, in the middle of the night, the phone rang. It was Betsy. "I just called to say I'm not coming home. I want to live my own life, my own way. I'm not coming home ever again."

Some of you know the pain that Ron and Marie experienced that night. You've received one of those calls too. Your son or daughter has chosen to leave home rather than be subject to life-as-usual in the family.

Runaways With Many Faces

Runaways are defined as young people who are away from home overnight without their parents' or guardians' permission. In his book *Runaway Kids: What Can You Do?*[3] Barry D. Mishkin says runaways fall into five categories:

1. Spontaneous unplanned episodes—where kids do a minimum of planning, stay away only a short time and voluntarily return home.

2. Deliberate successful episodes—where kids make deliberate, careful preparation and stay away longer periods of time. Sometimes the police become involved.

3. Temporary good-time escapades—where hedonistic good times are the motivation for running away. The runaway travels to "fun" places and tends to return voluntarily (usually broke).

4. Difficult long-term escapist episodes—where kids are attempting to escape a difficult home situation. Of this number, 36 percent run to escape physical or sexual abuse. Only 50 percent of these kids ever return home.

5. Temporary escapist episodes from unpleasant home situations—similar to number four but the runaway intends to stay away only for a few days; usually goes to a friend's house.

Running away is a serious problem in our anxiety-filled society. One out of every seven children will run away before age 18.[4]

Teenagers frequently believe running away is their only escape. Sometimes we all feel like that, don't we? And many of us during our growing-up years have either run away from home or at least thought about it.

I remember the day I ran away. I decided life would be much better on my own. So, at the wise old age of nine, I took a plastic bag and put into it everything a boy needed—my toothbrush and toothpaste and other essentials. Once packed, I tied the bag to the back of my bicycle and sped down the highway. With the wind at my back and a look of determination on my face, I was running away, never to return home again.

I suppose I got a quarter of a mile down the road before the spokes on my bicycle wore a hole in the plastic bag. I looked behind me in horror. There was a trail of toothpaste all the way up the highway. Worse than Hansel and Gretel, you could have followed me anywhere. Embarrassed and humiliated, I returned home, never to run away again.

I was a runaway of the first category. My escape had little planning, I only stayed away a short time and I voluntarily returned home. The prodigal in Jesus' family portrait was much different. He did not spontaneously leave home; he planned it for a long time. He did not escape from physical abuse or a bad home situation; he simply craved the good life. He wanted to try everything. He wanted to have fun. He was a category three runaway.

Attitudes always lead to actions. The younger son's selfish attitudes soon drove him to a selfish action—running away from home. Jesus told the story this way. "Not long after that, the younger son got together all he had, set off for a distant country and there squandered his wealth in wild living" (Luke 15:13).

Maybe It's Your Fault

Do you have a runaway? This heartache may have come as a result of inadequate parenting. You were guilty of inappropriate actions at home. You admit it. You're sorry about it. It was your fault. You told your daughter she was lazy. You said your son would never amount to anything. You were always on their case about something. Now you realize just how much you verbally abused your children. You called them stupid. You know exactly why they bolted from your house. They didn't want to get away from home; they wanted to get away from you. Now it's up to you to deal with your sin before God.

But 1 John 1:9–10 still works: "If we confess our sins, he is faithful and just and will forgive us our sins and purify us from all unrighteousness. If we claim we have not sinned, we make him out to be a liar and his word has no place in our lives." Admitting you have wronged your teenager and asking God to forgive you are the first steps in restoring your runaway.

Others of you have been kind and gracious to your kids. Your conscience is clear before God in the way you raised them. You weren't a perfect parent, of course, but you did your best. You treated your teen with respect and compassion.

Still, your son or daughter was like the prodigal in Jesus' story. He or she was unreasonable and arrogant. You felt the percussion as the door slammed in your face. You heard your child's vow never to return. "I don't love you" still rings in your ears. It hurts.

Many psychologists believe the pain of losing a son or daughter in death may not equal the pain of losing one to the world. Clearly the pain is just as real, and just as sharp.

If you have a runaway prodigal, there's hope for you. In telling this parable Jesus offered that hope. If the hard shell of this selfish son can be cracked by God, there's hope that the hard shell of your son or daughter will be cracked as well.

A Deliberate Departure

This prodigal had a natural dislike for the order and discipline of his home. Already tarnished by selfishness, he may also have been tainted with animosity toward his father and jealousy toward his older brother. He longed for the freedom of being on his own. He hankered for those lustful things he knew his father would never permit in his house. His head became dizzied with visions of what could be, if he was only on his own.

He thought about running away for a long time, but he lacked the resources. When the inheritance money surfaced, however, the last obstacle to his freedom was removed. Now bankrolled to fulfill his wildest dreams, he wasted no time in leaving home.

It's important to note that the prodigal did not stray away from home; he ran away from home. In the parable of the lost sheep, the sheep wandered aimlessly away from the shepherd. It was lost through foolishness. In the parable of the lost coin, the coin was accidentally dropped by the woman. It was lost through carelessness. But in the parable of the lost son, there was no wandering, no accidental disappearance. The younger son deliberately left home. He was lost through his own rebellion.

The prodigal left home and family, but he took everything else with him. All the money from his inheritance was in the pouch he carried on his fateful journey.

Apparently the boy had little head for business. He should have invested some of his capital where he was best known—his hometown. If he lost the rest of his inheritance on his journey, he would have a nest egg to fall back on. But this prodigal was no Harvard MBA and foolishly took all his money with him.

Taking all the inheritance signaled much more to his father. It meant the boy had little heart for his family. He was saying to his father, "There, I'm finally rid of you. Don't stay up nights looking for me. I won't be back!"

The prodigal burned his bridges. There was no reason for him to return. His selfish attitude turned into selfish action, and the language of leaving frequently translates, "I don't love you anymore!"

Journey to a Far Country

The Master Storyteller said the younger son journeyed into a far country. But where would a young Jewish boy run from the Promised Land? Perhaps to Carthage on the north coast of Africa. A Roman colony was thriving there. Or maybe Athens, the world center of culture and the arts. And let's not forget Rome, the capital of the Empire. That was the place to seek fame and fortune. He could lose himself in the glitz and glamour of the big city. Every kind of wanton pleasure could be bought in Rome. The young prodigal now had plenty of cash; maybe Rome was where he went.

It doesn't matter actually. This is a parable. Exact details are not important. It's the underlying truth that's important. But notice that this lad didn't just go across the street; he got as far from his father as those prodigal feet could take him. He journeyed to a distant land.

So, now what? What happens to runaways when they leave home? That usually depends on why they run away, and what awaits their return.

43% of homeless youth were asked to leave home by a parent.

14.7 years is the average age of a runaway, homeless youth.

60% of runaways have experienced physical or sexual abuse.

52% of homeless youth have been assaulted on the streets.

Source: YouthCare, 2500 NE 54th Street, Suite 100, Seattle, WA 98105

Why Kids Run

Some runaways are known as "push-outs" because they've been forced by their parents or guardians to leave. Their conduct at home has been an irritant to their parents. There was constant conflict in the home. The family was happy to see them go. They were pushed out.

Others are called "throwaways" because they've left home with the approval of their parents. The family no longer wants them. Running is their way of searching for someone to love them.

Julie is a young woman who listens to *Back to the Bible*. She has written to us on several occasions for counsel and advice. Recently she wrote:

"I have always lived in sadness. It's an emotion I know real well.

"I'm in my late 20s. I never knew my dad, and I've come to realize what I missed growing up without him. I wrote to a convent, begging them to let me become a nun and live in a sheltered world, just to get away from an alcoholic mom, a violent brother and a cold sister. The convent didn't want me.

"I'm so desperate for love. I came close to killing myself. The razor was in my hand. I hate pain. I hate the feeling of being unloved when you so desperately need love."

You don't have to read between the lines to feel Julie's pain. For some people like Julie, running turns the unloved slave into the master of their own fate. Initially it opens all the right doors and closes all the deep wounds. But it doesn't last.

Running away from home has a treasured history. Remember Mark Twain's runaway hero—Huckleberry Finn? Huck ran away, not to enjoy the adventures on the Mississippi River but to escape the cruel treatment of his father. He was kidnapped from his foster home in Hannibal, Missouri. His father locked Huck in a cabin in the woods. It is from this kind of abuse that the young boy fled.

Typically those who run away from such treatment never return home again. The cruelty and deprivation of the streets is no worse—and often better—than what they experienced at home.

For whatever reason, kids run. They run from the rules and old-fashioned ideas of their parents. They run from the truth.

Some run from pain and abuse. But if our kids think that beneath everything there's a genuine warmth and love at home, they'll come back. That's why what awaits kids if they return is so important to the runaway.

What's a Parent to Do?

If your child has left home, they need to believe there's genuine compassion awaiting them when they return. Their return may depend on it. But only you, Dad and Mom, can assure that compassion awaits your runaway. It's the only way to survive the prodigals in your life.

In her book *Runaways*, Lillian Ambrosino says, "Some parents will not let their children return. They are angry at the thwarting of their authority, the 'insolence.' Just as children want to punish their parents, some parents, too, want to hurt their children."[5]

If this is true with you, it's an unhealthy attitude that must be left on the altar of God. Your child may have hurt you deeply with an "I don't love you anymore" slam of the door, but your response cannot be to get even with them.

As Jesus' parable unfolds we are struck with how very different the father's reaction was from those parents who want to punish their children. The prodigal ran away, but he knew he could return. He didn't deserve it, but deep down inside he believed that if he ever came home again, a loving father would be waiting for him. He was!

You face some hard questions if you have a runaway prodigal. Ask yourself, "What have I done that may have contributed to my teen running away?" "If they ever want to come back, will they find a compassionate welcome or just another lecture?" "What do I think my teen expects if they come home again?"

When the door slams and you know that means "I don't love you anymore," it hurts. But you, parents, hold the key to healing those hurt relationships. Here's what you can do.

First, begin with yourself. Confess to God anything that needs confession. Don't be shortsighted. Rarely are any of us completely innocent. Ask God to show you specifically where you may have contributed to the tension in your home. Ask Him to work in your heart so you can be the kind of parent the father was in Jesus' parable. If you are not, your runaway will never want to come home again.

Then, call the police and report your teen missing. If you live in America, call the National Runaway Hotline at 1-800-621-4000. The National Runaway Switchboard's address is: 3080 North Lincoln Avenue, Chicago, IL 60651. Or contact the National Center for Missing & Exploited Children at 1-800-THE LOST or 703-274-3900. They are located at: Charles B. Wang International Children's Building, 699 Prince Street, Alexandria, VA 22314. Take positive steps to get your teen back.

And don't forget to pray for your runaway. Pray that God will protect them on the streets. Pray that He will deliver them from the evil one (Matt. 6:13). Pray that His guardian angels will keep them from falling into deep and damaging sin while they are living their prodigal lifestyle (Ps. 91:11-13). Ask others to pray with you. Get serious about prayer. It's the strongest weapon you have against Satan. Wield the sword of prayer skillfully and often.

Runaways do come home. Eventually the prodigal son in Jesus' parable came back. There's real reason for you to hope. Pave the way for your son or daughter to return. Commit them to God and wait. Prodigals do come home again. Pray that yours will in the perfect timing of God. Hold onto this hope.

Additional sources of help online:

Child Quest Int'l — http://www.childquest.org

Child Search — http://www.childsearch.org

Missing Children — Net Central —
http://www.child.net/missing.htm

Child Watch of North America —
http://www.childwatch.org

Polly Klass Foundation —
http://www.pollyklass.org

Child Find Canada — http://www.childfind.ca

Notes

1. National Runaway Switchboard, nrscrisisline.org
2. YouthCare. Info@youthcare.org
3. Barry D. Mishkin. *Runaway Kids: What Can You Do?* (Dayton, OH: P.P.I. Publishing Co., 1983), 35.
4. National Runaway Switchboard, nrscrisisline.org
5. Lillian Ambrosino. *Runaways.* (Boston: Beacon Press, 1971), 5.

Chapter 3

NO FUN IN THE CITY

"A bag with holes"

Freedom can be a very exhilarating thing!

On August 13, 1961, the East German government was busy. Overnight they built a wall nearly 12 feet high and 3,937 feet long. It was called the Berlin Wall because it closed the border between East Berlin and West Berlin. More than a quarter of a century later, who can forget those German faces in November 1989 as young and old alike gleefully smashed that wall with their own hammers and picks. Or when more than 50 American hostages were freed from the U.S. Embassy in Tehran after being held captive for 444 days. Their smiles and tears became forever etched on our minds. Freedom is a powerful stimulant.

Still, freedom carries with it a heavy price tag—not just to win but to maintain. In Jesus' family portrait, the father paid a heavy price to give his young son freedom. It cost him the premature dispersal of the family inheritance. It also cost him a son, but maybe not the one you think.

Once the prodigal arrived in that distant land, he also experienced the cost of freedom. Freedom is encumbered with significant responsibility. The prodigal learned the hard way that while he was ready for freedom, he was not ready for the responsibility that freedom brings.

Many runaways discover the same thing. Once they've left home they learn three important facts about life: First, what money they have doesn't go very far. Second, without money, a warm bed is hard to come by. And third, there's not a refrigerator on every corner.

This is quite a shock for most teen runaways because they tend to be very idealistic like the prodigal. They are not poor, underprivileged kids. In fact, 80 percent of the runaways in America are white and come from middle or upper middle-class families. The majority are starved for affection, not for food. They bolt from their home to find love, not fortune. But what they find is anything but affection.

What Is a Prodigal?

Why do we refer to Jesus' story as the parable of the prodigal son? What is a prodigal anyway?

The word *prodigal* means "extravagant, someone who is lavish with his or her resources." That could be a good thing. God was lavish with the resources of His love and grace. But the word also means "recklessly wasteful, someone who is a spendthrift."

Did you notice that the word *prodigal* does not mean someone who runs away from home. It's from Jesus' parable and the fact that the younger son leaves home that the word takes on the connotation of a runaway. But you don't have to run away to be a prodigal. Lots of prodigals remain at home. In fact, before Jesus finishes painting His family portrait, He'll introduce us to a second prodigal son, the one who never left home.

But the younger son in Jesus' story is the classic example of a prodigal. Once in a far country you'd expect the prodigal to indulge himself a bit and spend a little money foolishly. He did. But after that initial rush, the smart thing would have been for him to invest his money. He didn't.

As Jesus continued to tell the parable, He said, "Not long after that, the younger son got together all he had, set off for a distant country and there squandered his wealth in wild living" (v. 13).

The prodigal didn't have a plan. He received no financial counsel from others. He did no estate planning. He had no stocks, bonds or mutual funds in his financial portfolio. There were no Swiss bank accounts. Nothing! He wasted everything, his entire inheritance. It was all gone!

Jesus chose a graphic word to picture the prodigal's waste. Elsewhere this verb is used of scattering grain. For example, in the parable of the talents, the lazy servant claimed he failed to invest his talent because his master was a hard man, gathering where he had not *scattered* seed (Matt. 25:24-26). Jesus used the same word for the prodigal's waste.

In predicting Peter's denial, Jesus quoted from Zechariah 13:7, "I will strike the shepherd, and the sheep will be scattered" (Mark 14:27). It's the same word as in Luke 15:13.

And Caiaphas the high priest prophesied that Jesus would die for the Jewish nation including "the scattered children of God" (John 11:52). Same word.

Jesus was saying that the boy let the father's money slip through his fingers. He wasted it, squandered it, scattered it like grain.

The prodigal had no experience in handling money. He simply spent his way into poverty. His life was one big party. Days and nights were filled with wild excitement of the least wholesome variety.

Choose any adjective you want—profligate, extravagant, excessive, lavish—they all describe the lifestyle of the rash and foolish.

Rejecting the Gift of God

It doesn't take a financial wizard to know that when your outgo exceeds your income, your upkeep will be your downfall. The prodigal's outgo was accelerated and his income was obliterated. That's a classic scenario for bankruptcy.

Spending money right and left is the surest way to have none left. This foolish son squandered his resources. Soon he was busted, broke, tapped out. He had no money at all. He was now destitute, discouraged and alone. The prodigal's self-interest led to self-destruction.

There's a great tragedy here beyond the dissipated life of the prodigal. An equal tragedy is what the lad did with the gift from God.

The money the prodigal foolishly squandered was his inheritance, converted to cash when his father sold some of the family land. That ancestral real estate was a gift to his tribe, and specifically to his family. In a very real sense, the prodigal carelessly squandered the gift of God to his ancestors.

But isn't that always true? When we squander our natural

resources, we squander a gift from God. When we abort our fetal children, we abort a gift from God. When men and women reject Jesus as their Savior, they reject the most precious gift of all from God. Anything of intrinsic value is a gift of God. To squander God's gifts isn't just foolish, it's criminal. Squandering the gifts of God is nothing less than sin.

Stewardship Versus Squandership

What God expects from us is stewardship, not squandership. It is required that stewards be faithful (1 Cor. 4:2), and that faithfulness extends to every aspect of life.

Pick an area, any area. God wants us to be faithful stewards. Our environment—trees, water, air, etc. We are stewards of these gifts from God and must faithfully preserve them. Our finances—paycheck, savings accounts, IRAs, etc. We are stewards of these gifts from God and must faithfully manage them. Our children—sons, daughters, grandchildren, etc. We are stewards of these gifts from God and must faithfully raise them.

All of life is a stewardship, and the prodigal miserably failed the test of stewardship. He wasted all God had given him through raucous living. He fled from his father to be free, to make his own decisions, to run his own life. In reality, his newfound freedom enslaved him to the worst form of bondage—the bondage of sin.

If this story ended right here, it would be a genuine tragedy. A young lad who had everything, and who lost it all. But that was inevitable. When we selfishly demand what we have no right to demand, it's inevitable that our resources will be wasted. Selfishness never prospers long, because God won't permit it to prosper.

Having always had things provided for him, having no experience in handling funds, the prodigal did what many people do. He allowed riches to ruin his life.

First, he failed to recognize that all he had came from God and belonged to God. He forgot the words of Job: "If I have put my trust in gold or said to pure gold, 'You are my security,' if I have rejoiced over my great wealth, the fortune my hands had gained . . . then these also would be sins to be judged, for I would have been unfaithful to God on high" (Job 31:24-25, 28). That's good advice for all of us.

In addition, the prodigal squandered God's great gift. He spent his money foolishly. As the prophet Haggai said, he had sown much but it brought in little. He ate, but he never seemed to have enough. He drank with the best of them, but he was never filled. He had money to buy fashionable and expensive clothes, but they did not keep him warm. He was like one who earned wages but put them into a bag with holes in it (Hag. 1:6).

Wasting God's Greatest Resource

We hear a lot today about wasted resources. Most of the talk relates to tangible things—wasted money, wasted food, wasted gasoline. Far more tragic is the waste of intangible, spiritual resources.

Love is a resource, but many confuse it with lust and waste it time after time with person after person. Health is a resource, but many abuse it with alcohol, drugs or overeating. Time is a resource, but many let it slip through their fingers with no eternal investment.

The greatest waste of all is the waste of God's great resource—His Son, Jesus Christ. How tragic to have a debt and no means to pay it. More tragic is to have someone pay our debt and not accept it.

Jesus Christ paid our debt for sin. He paid it with His blood. He is our salvation. What a waste of resources to have the blood of Jesus Christ as a covering for sin and not ask Him to apply it.

Don't waste this precious resource as you think about this dysfunctional family in Jesus' parable. It's the only resource that can make you a part of the family of God.

FINDING YOUR WAY HOME
Billy Buckley

Billy Buckley was a good kid—the kind that everybody liked. He grew up in a Christian home and was saved as a young boy while attending the Good News Club at his school. But attending church was a chore for him. It wasn't as exciting as video games. He went because his mother dragged him there. At age 13 he was baptized, but no one ever took the time to disciple Billy.

His story is typical. Good kid. Saved at an early age. Attended church but never grew to spiritual maturity. He was a statistic, a number on the church roll. He was not a growing Christian; he was a going Christian—going to church week after week with little impact on his life

Finally, as a teenager, Billy had enough. He wanted out. "I decided to put this church thing behind me for good," says Billy. "I was emotionally stretched in many different directions. I knew enough of God's Word to know what I ought to do, but not enough to make me want to do it." His emotional state was fragile. He needed something—a crutch—something to lead him out of his emotional malaise.

Bottoms Up

That's when Billy made the mistake of his life. He turned to alcohol to ease his emotional pain. He found his way out at the bottom of a bottle.

As Billy retells his story: "When I first discovered alcohol, I thought I had found the answer to all my inadequacies. I was bigger, stronger, tougher, friendlier, better looking, and all those other 'er's' you can think of." Alcohol does that to a person. It makes them something they are not. Sadly, it also robs them of who and what they are.

Billy's drinking worsened each year. It led him to meet the wrong people, at the wrong places, for the wrong reasons. In his drunken state Billy often met girls who were also in the wrong place for the wrong reason. But as Billy eventually learned, alcohol and sex are not only a dangerous combination but also unsatisfying.

Billy's life continued to be empty, fruitless, meaningless. He was miserable, and the more miserable he became, the more he drank. It was an endless cycle of misery and pain, lubricated with alcohol.

Eventually his drinking resulted in physical deterioration and broken relationships, and Billy found himself emotionally and spiritually bankrupt. What he turned to for comfort, strength and hope suddenly turned on him. Instead of relieving his agony, it only intensified all that original pain and added much more.

"I Just Wanted to Die"

"At my darkest hour," says Billy, "I just wanted to die and finally be rid of all the hurt I had carried for so many years."

It's a story retold every day of the week. But it's such an avoidable story. If only Billy had worked on his relationship with God, he wouldn't have needed to work on the south end of a whisky bottle. Billy wandered away from the life of his family. He disappointed his mother. He ruined his life. He was a classic prodigal. And now he wanted to die.

But God wouldn't let him die. Instead, God brought a friend into Billy's life who had been down that same path as our prodigal. She was now sober and wanted to help Billy dry out too.

How well Billy remembers those days of despair and nights of nausea. He recalls, "Struggling with sobriety and angry with God for allowing all this pain in my life, I started to talk to Him out loud. I told God I didn't trust Him, and that I was afraid of Him because of all the horrible things I had done."

Billy didn't know it at the time, but he had just taken a giant step on the road that leads home. He had cried out to God in his anguish and despair, and God said, "I didn't go anywhere, I'm right here. I never abandoned you. In those dark hours, I was there. You just needed to turn around and look for Me."

That's what Billy wanted. He wanted to go home—home to his family and, more than anything, home to God. In Billy's own words: "Suddenly I was broken and humbled. Reduced to tears, I confessed all the sin I could remember that day. I turned that anger, hurt and loneliness over to my Lord and Savior. He filled the void, welcomed me back with open arms and poured His love out on me."

Feeling at Home in the Family

That was the beginning of the end for Billy the prodigal. Just like the young lad in Jesus' parable, Billy came to his senses. He realized what a fool he had been and he wanted to come back to the Father.

Billy is now at home in the family of God. His life is so different, so blessed, so worth living. For him, alcohol was his pigpen experience. It's what dragged him down to the bottom of his personal pit, but that's where he discovered God. The Father welcomed him with open arms, hugged him and kissed him. Billy would never be the same again.

Now Billy freely testifies to others of God's grace and goodness in his life. "God has blessed me in so many ways since then. I am married to a lovely woman who loves God. I am active in my church, answered the call to go on short-term missions trips, and now involved in a full-time ministry. I also enjoy a close personal relationship with my Lord. I know now that God didn't put me in that personal hell, but He did open the gates and let me out!"

Billy the (prodigal) kid is now Billy the useful servant of the Lord. What made the difference? Billy knows. "Simply giving in to the love of the Heavenly Father. When a prodigal comes to grips with the love of God in his or her life, the prodigal lifestyle doesn't stand a chance. Nothing is as powerful or as attractive as the love of God. I know. I've been there."

Chapter 4

GOD'S INCREDIBLE TIMING

"Timing is everything!"

You can survive the prodigals in your life if you learn to tell time by God's clock. If you don't, you'll sit up nights worrying for no reason at all. Survive your prodigal by yielding to God's incredible timing.

In 1832 he was a candidate for his state legislature. He lost! In 1834 he again ran and this time won. In 1847 he was elected to the United States Congress, but only served one term. He wasn't even renominated by his own party! He campaigned for Zachary Taylor for President, hoping to be appointed Commissioner of the General Land Office. He wasn't! Defeated, he returned to his law practice.

In 1854 he again ran for his state legislature and won. But he resigned, hoping the new anti-Nebraska party would support him for the United States Senate. They didn't!

In 1856 he was nominated for the office of Vice President of the United States. He lost! In 1858 again he ran for the U.S. Senate. Again he lost!

In 1860 he was simply nominated as a favorite son from the state of Illinois, and later that year Abraham Lincoln was elected the 16th President of the United States of America.

God wanted Abraham Lincoln to serve the United States as President, but only in His timing, not in Lincoln's timing. There was no use sitting up nights worrying about it. All Lincoln had to do was go about his life and wait for God's perfect timing.

The same thing is true for us today. If you're to survive a prodigal in your life, you must keep your eyes on the timetable of God, for only then will you keep perfect time.

Life for the prodigal son was on a downward spiral. He had left home and now lost everything. He was all alone and penniless. He got together all he had when he left home (v. 13); he spent all he had on his prodigal lifestyle (v. 14). The double use of the word *all* is no coincidence. He took all he had; he squandered all he had.

Dual Disasters

Two disasters struck the prodigal almost simultaneously. The first he was responsible for; the second he was not. His prodigal life drained all his funds. At the same time a severe famine struck the land. The runaway son faced the two-sided dilemma of too little funds and too much famine.

The prodigal certainly experienced a famine of frills. He had been living extravagantly, but the penthouse was now gone and the city mission would be his next address if he didn't return home soon. And he undoubtedly experienced a famine of friends. Proverbs 19:4 is right. "Wealth brings many friends." When the prodigal's wealth was gone, his newfound friends were swept away with it.

While he must have experienced these peripheral kinds of famine, what Jesus obviously had in mind was a literal, bone-crunching famine of food. This was a real famine, a serious problem for any prodigal pauper.

Sometimes famines are depicted in the Bible as instruments of God's punishment (cf. Lev. 26:19ff.; 2 Kings 8:1; Ezek. 5:16; et al.). But in this case, the famine was more of an attention-getter than a judgment. God wanted to get the attention of this wayward son, and the famine came at a time which had the most dramatic effect on him. Such is the incredible timing of God.

No Coincidence

Verse 14 says, "After he had spent everything, there was a severe famine in that whole country, and he began to be in need." The prodigal was to be blamed for spending all, but not for the arrival of the mighty famine. The two events are not related in his thinking, but they are clearly related in God's timing.

Is this mere coincidence? Was it a cruel twist of fate that brought a famine at precisely the moment the prodigal went broke? Hardly. What do you suppose the odds are that a young man, who had never seen starvation in his life, would be in a distant country at pre-cisely the same time a severe famine devastated that land? And even more incredibly, what are the odds that this would occur immedi-ately after the prodigal just finished squandering his portion of the family fortune? I'd say the odds are too great to be believable. This is a dramatic display of the awesome timing of God. So incredible is God's timing that compared to it, Greenwich Mean Time (GMT) is child's play.

This was not the first time. Think about it. There had been events before this one that evidenced the incredible timing of God.

God Is Always on Time

When a famine threatened to exterminate the descendants of His chosen nation—Israel, God had a man in a position to save them all. Although Joseph had been sold into slavery, he became Prime Minister of Egypt. In the perfect timing of God, Joseph's brothers were forced to come to him for food (Gen. 37-50) and he spared their lives. That's the perfect timing of God.

An evil villain wanted to exterminate the entire Jewish population of ancient Persia. Haman would have been successful, too, had it not been for the perfect timing of God. A Jewess named Esther became Queen of the Persian Empire and was able to influence the king to rescind the death warrant on the Jews. "And who knows but that you have come to a royal position for such a time as this?" (Esther 4:14). That's the perfect timing of God.

The first-century church was almost entirely Jewish in member-ship, and yet Gentiles were being saved in large numbers. A split in the church was inevitable unless someone could bridge the gap between the Jews and the Gentiles. That someone would have to be a Jew—a true Jew, not a proselyte. But he would also need to have a burden for the Gentiles. That's a pretty tall order. It seemed impos-sible to find such a person when the Pharisee Saul was saved and became the Apostle Paul. That's the perfect timing of God.

Even our Savior was born "when the time had fully come" (Gal. 4:4). The world needed Him for centuries, but Jesus Christ was born the Babe in Bethlehem's stable on a night God determined before the world began. That's the perfect timing of God.

The prodigal left home and journeyed into a distant land. No famine. He lived it up and enjoyed the financial benefits of his ancestor's inheritance. No famine. But when he squandered his money and found himself broke, suddenly a severe famine blanketed the land. That's the perfect timing of God.

Had the famine come while the prodigal was still at home, it would have had no impact on him. Had it come when he still had lots of money, he could have bought his way out of it. But God kept perfect time for this prodigal. He knows how to keep perfect time for your prodigal too.

A Time for Every Purpose

"There is a time for everything, and a season for every activity under heaven" (Eccl. 3:1).

There is a time to be born and a time to die. There is a time to plant and a time to reap. There is a time to weep and a time to laugh. Listen to me. There is a time to run away from home and there is a time to return home again. There is a time for everything, and a season for every activity under heaven.

I don't know what God's purpose is in your life. If you have a runaway child, I don't know what His purpose is in your child's life. If you have experienced the pain of a prodigal spouse, I don't know what God's purpose is in your spouse's life. But I do know this. There is a season for every activity under heaven and a purpose for everything.

In His time, God will make all things beautiful. In His time, God will show you the purpose for your teenager slamming the door in your face and leaving home. In His time, God will heal the emotional wounds you have experienced through the dark days of your life. But you have to wait for His time.

God's perfect timing doesn't always occur in Eastern Standard Time (EST) or Pacific Standard Time (PST). But it always occurs in DST (Divine Standard Time). God is never early, never late. He is supra time, above time, beyond time. When the perfect, eternal, omniscient God moves in your prodigal's life, He'll do so with perfect timing. How could He do less?

52

Pray for your prodigal. Do all you can to get them to come back. But remember, it will only happen in God's timing. Adjust yourself to His timing. It's the only way to survive the prodigals in your life.

Waiting is the hardest thing in the world, but you can't speed up God's timetable. What you can do is commit yourself to it. Commit your prodigals to His timetable as well.

Give Him time. He'll do what's best; just give Him time.

Chapter 5

NEED A LITTLE HELP
FROM MY FRIENDS

"I can make it on my own"

"Life is a tale, told by an idiot, full of sound and fury, signifying nothing."[1]

Do you recognize those words? That line from *Macbeth* (Act V, Scene 5) well describes how the prodigal son felt. His life was filled with a great big empty, a whole bunch of nothing. He had come to the end of his rope.

Most runaways find themselves where the prodigal son found himself. They quickly spend every penny they have and turn to life on the streets. Too often for teenagers, male and female, that means prostitution. For others it means peddling drugs or meaningless minimum-wage jobs. This comes as a result of a prevailing attitude among prodigals—"I can make it on my own."

The prodigal spent his wad on good-time living with bad-time results. Now he was busted, with no money and nothing to eat. In a faraway land, he was all by himself, with no one to turn to.

Taking Charge

And that's the problem. The prodigal had nowhere to turn, so he did what prodigals do. He turned inward. He turned to himself and his own resources to get him out of his jam. That only got him in deeper. In one way or another, we've all experienced this dilemma.

Listen to what Jesus said about the prodigal in Luke 15:14-16, "After he had spent everything, there was a severe famine in that whole country, and he began to be in need. So he went and hired himself out to a citizen of that country, who sent him to his fields to feed pigs. He longed to fill his stomach with the pods that the pigs were eating, but no one gave him anything."

Now what? The prodigal was broke. A debilitating famine had arrived. Would he realize now how good he had it back home with his father? Would he swallow his pride and return home? Not a chance! He was still convinced he didn't need his father or his family.

All he needed was a break. If he could just find a job and get some quick cash, he was convinced he could make it on his own.

We prodigals are always that way, aren't we? When we wander from God and from the life of His family, we never return until there are no other alternatives. As long as we think we can make it on our own, our first thought is to take charge ourselves.

Runaways are that way too. Being far from home and penniless never seems to be sufficient reason to pack it in and go home again. When a prodigal spouse leaves the family for more fulfilling pastures, being lonely and disappointed never seem to be enough to bring repentance and return. As long as they feel they can dig themselves out of the mess they've made of their lives, as long as they think their big break is just around the corner, they'll do anything to keep from going back.

All prodigals are the same. Like the prodigal son, they try to find the strength within themselves to keep on going, keep on living, keep on running, keep on sinning.

The Insufficiency of Self-Sufficiency

But surely we don't object if the prodigal got a job and took care of himself. That reflects the Puritan work ethic, doesn't it? Isn't finding work and paying your bills better than relying on the welfare system to do it for you? What's wrong with what the prodigal did?

On the surface, nothing. It even appears to be commendable. When he came to the end of his rope, he tied a knot and hung on. But this betrayed a lingering refusal to recognize his sin. He continued to shut God out of his life.

In fact, have you noticed that God didn't figure in the prodigal's thinking at all. Nowhere did it cross his mind that he was wrong. He never considered his mistreatment of his father. His only concern was himself. He was convinced he didn't need to go home; he could make it on his own.

But isn't that the way many people are today? They say they don't need God. They don't need the church. They don't care about heaven or hell. Just listen to them: "I'm the captain of my ship; I'm the master of my fate. Nobody tells me what to do. If I mess up my life, there will be no one but me to blame." In fact, I've heard people hold that belief right up to the day they took their own lives in despair.

Get a Job

The prodigal's solution to being penniless and hungry was to find a job. Likely he combed the help-wanted ads in the paper and used the shoe leather express in pursuit of work.

But times were tough. There was a famine. Jobs were not easy to come by. He had no references. His only qualification was being the son of a wealthy landowner. He didn't stand much of a chance. What kind of a job could he get?

In His parable, Jesus referred to the older brother working in his father's fields, but He never mentioned the younger son working. Perhaps this boy wasn't accustomed to hard work. The prodigal must now do for a stranger what there is no record he ever did for his father. He went to work. He hired on with a pig farmer to feed the pigs. Jesus said, "So he went and hired himself out to a citizen of that country."

The verb Jesus chose means to *glue together*. In the New Testament this verb only occurs in the passive voice. That means the prodigal was glued to his employer, or glued himself to his employer. It was not something he wanted to happen; it was something that had to happen. This boy was thoroughly dependent on the good graces of this pig farmer.

Ironic, isn't it, that the young man who ran away from home to be independent was now glued to a stranger. Ironic, too, that the prodigal son, who wanted nothing to do with work on the farm, was now working on a farm. This selfish boy was climbing the social ladder, but in reverse.

The Ultimate Humiliation

Perhaps the most ironic thing is that the farmer sent the prodigal into his fields to feed pigs. Imagine the irony of a Jewish boy feeding the pigs. For a Jew, no occupation could have been more humiliating, more dreadful, more distasteful.

There is an old rabbinical saying, "Cursed be the man who would breed swine." As an unclean animal, the levitical Law absolutely forbade Jews to eat swine (Lev. 11:7). They regarded the pig as an abomination, but the prodigal's life had become so abominable itself, he gladly hired on to feed the pigs.

Was this just a cruel twist of fate? Was this a divine joke? Not at all. This parable was told by the Master Storyteller. Jesus had a clear lesson for all prodigals.

When we wander from God, we meander into meaninglessness. The prodigal son was convinced he could make it on his own, but instead he sank deep into the emptiness of aimlessness. His life was going nowhere fast. He didn't know where he was headed. The fact is, he was headed nowhere.

The Empty-Stomach Syndrome

Let's not lose sight of the fact that once the hungry lad hired on with the pig farmer, he had a job but he still had no food. His stomach growled so loudly even the pigs must have glared at him. The hog husks began to look curiously appetizing. If he could have gotten away with it, the prodigal would have eaten those pig pods, but no one gave him any.

Add humiliation to hunger. When you're running from God, troubles do seem to multiply, don't they?

These husks were not from corn but more likely were pods from the carob tree. Carob pods look remarkably like a flattened, dried banana. Today carob is called "the poor man's chocolate," but in ancient times these pods were considered the poorest food, used only to feed animals.

There is an interesting rabbinical statement something to the effect, "When the Israelites are reduced to carob pods, then they repent." Could this be true of the prodigal son? Was it time that he repented of his foolish behavior?

It's always time to repent of foolish behavior, and the boy did.

But before he repented, the prodigal first did what the world advises us to do in similar situations. He looked within himself to find the strength to go on. He looked to his own resources. He was still trying to make it on his own. He's the perfect example of the worldly fool.

The world says you don't need God; you are all the god you need. Look inside yourself. There you will find the strength to go on. There you will find your source. There you will find god. But the world is wrong.

The Emptiness of Aimlessness

Johann Wolfgang von Goethe said, "A useless life is only an early death." Feeding the pigs must have caused this prodigal to die a thousand deaths. He had wandered into a life of emptiness. For him, life was just as Shakespeare described it: "a tale, told by an idiot, full of sound and fury, signifying nothing."

Does the prodigal's life parallel your life? Are you wandering in the emptiness of aimlessness? Perhaps you're trapped in a dead-end job, going nowhere. Have you drifted from God and now find yourself working day after day for someone you don't even care about? Are you laboring for the husks of life, the dregs at the bottom of the cup? Has work lost meaning for you, just as life has?

"The great use of life is to spend it for something that outlasts it," said William James. Are you satisfied just to work for the present, rather than to build for the future?

If so, you're living the life of the prodigal son and you may not even know it. Come to grips with your life and your future. Ask yourself if you have wandered away from your Heavenly Father. Are you trying to survive a prodigal only to find out you're a spiritual prodigal yourself? It's a startling revelation, but it's just such emptiness at home that drives some kids to seek meaning elsewhere.

Come to yourself and find the road back to God. Before he came to himself, the prodigal son had a bright future behind him. Don't let this be said of you.

Without God, Without Meaning

Prodigals have a natural bent to stay "at large" as long as they can.

They don't want to crawl back home and they don't intend to. Your prodigal will be like that.

What fools we are when we look inward. Self-sufficiency cannot cure the loneliness of prodigalism. There's nothing in us that can take away our emptiness. There is nothing inside that can give direction to our aimlessness. There is nothing in there that can give purpose to our meaninglessness.

Unless your prodigal looks to the father, the Heavenly Father from whom they have run, they will continue wandering without purpose. Even if they strike it rich and there seems to be a turnaround in their luck, they'll still be empty. There is a big God-shaped void in each of our lives. We'll not fill it by looking inward, only by looking upward.

The prodigal son would feel right at home with the New Age thinkers today. He looked inward for strength, rather than upward. He had come to the end of his resources, but he continued to look to himself for his salvation. He was disappointed, just as everyone is who looks within for help. Our only help comes from outside us, not from within us. The psalmist was right when he said, "I will lift up my eyes to the hills—where does my help come from? My help comes from the LORD, the Maker of heaven and earth" (Ps. 121:1).

A Neurosis of Emptiness

Psychiatrist Carl Jung noted that psychiatrists who are not superficial have come to the conclusion that the vast neurotic misery of the world could be termed a neurosis of emptiness. Men cut themselves off from the root of their being, from God, and then life turns empty, inane, meaningless, without purpose.

Jung concluded that when God goes, goals go. When goals go, meaning goes. When meaning goes, value goes, and the end result is the experience of the prodigal—the emptiness of aimlessness.

Many people have wandered into this emptiness, just like the prodigal. Perhaps your son or daughter is one of them. They're living in loneliness, finding little meaning in their lives.

But aimlessness is a two-way street. Some parents of prodigals have drifted into aimlessness as well. Their lives were emptied of meaning when their prodigal slammed the door behind them.

If you're one of those parents, isn't it time you threw away the pods of your life and exchanged them for the blessing of God? Isn't it time you allowed some meaning back into your life?

If you aren't a Christian, that's where you need to begin.

Don't look inside yourself for strength to tough out your loneliness. Look to the Lord Jesus. He died at Calvary to pay the penalty for your sin. He rose from the dead to give your life eternal meaning. If you believe your sin can be forgiven by trusting Jesus as your Savior, ask Him to save you. He will.

All who seek meaning only in their children suffer a severe crisis of meaning when those children depart. But not the Christian. Sure it hurts when our kids become prodigals, but that doesn't drive us to an empty existence. It doesn't rob us of personal meaning.

If you're feeling a lack of acceptance by your prodigal, don't search for acceptance within yourself. You'll only be disappointed. You can't make it on your own through these days of anguish any more than your prodigal can. The emptiness in your life can be eradicated, but only by Jesus Christ. Give your feelings, your family, your future to Him. Ask Him to give you significance and a feeling of purpose. He will; He really will.

Notes

1. William Shakespeare. *The Tragedy of Macbeth* in The Yale Shakespeare, Revised Edition. (New Haven: Yale University Press, 1954).

Chapter 6

GOOD-TIME LIVING
BAD-TIME RESULTS

"What a fool I've been"

The great Baptist preacher of the 19th century, Charles Haddon Spurgeon, loved to tell the story of old Betty. Old Betty became a Christian late in her life. Being poor and uneducated there wasn't much Betty could do for the Lord, but she did what she could.

Old Betty visited the sick. She collected money from friends and gave it to the poor. Sometimes she gave out of her own poverty to those poorer still. Always she told of God's love and grace in saving her.

When old Betty caught a cold and became afflicted with rheumatism, her health began to deteriorate severely. For months she lay in bed, her body racked with pain. Betty's condition appeared to be hopeless.

One day a minister came to visit old Betty. Knowing how active she had been for the Lord, the preacher asked if she found it difficult just lying there in bed. Betty replied, "Oh, not at all. When I was well, I used to hear the Lord say, 'Betty, go here. Betty, go there. Betty, do this. Betty, do that.' And now I hear Him say, 'Betty, lie still and cough.'"

Bitter or Better?

Remarkable, isn't it, how affliction and adversity affect us. Some become bitter through adversity; some become better.

Betty clearly became better. Which is true of you?

Having spent all and suffered the deprivation of famine, having been humiliated by feeding the pigs, the prodigal son reeled in painful adversity. He was hungry, dirty and in despair. The runaway had no friends, no food, no frills. He was broke and tired, and about to do the right thing—finally!

Luke 15:17 is the turning point in the prodigal's story. In fact, what happens in verse 17 is the turning point in the lives of many people.

Here's what Jesus said. "When he came to his senses, he said, 'How many of my father's hired men have food to spare, and here I am starving to death!'"

The prodigal made a colossal self-discovery. His father's hired servants had it much better than he did. How could this be? Had the prodigal missed something? Had he violated some inviolate law of God? Finally the prodigal's twisted thinking was beginning to straighten out.

Straight Thinking

The runaway boy saw the mistake he made. He wised up. He came to himself. When he finally saw what a fool he had been, then and only then, he decided that his life was not better off now than it had been at home.

The prodigal was reaping what he sowed, but for the first time in this parable there is light at the end of the tunnel. He came to his senses. He had a change of mind. Isn't that what repentance means—a change of mind? The prodigal son had been a fool; now he was repenting of his foolishness and reevaluating his relationship with his father.

As he fed the carob pods to the pigs, the prodigal's mind drifted back to his home and father. He remembered just how good he really had it back there. He thought of his warm bed and the conversations around the dinner table. His life hadn't been perfect back home and he knew it. But in comparison to this pig lot, home was heaven.

But notice what really got to him? It was the thought of his father's hired servants. They had all the food they needed and more, and he was dying of hunger. It wasn't his sin that brought the prodigal to himself; it was his stomach. Hardship has a way of making us face the facts, especially stomach facts.

That's why we should never ask God to spare our prodigals from tough times. We ask Him to preserve their lives, but not keep them from difficulty. Without difficulty they rarely learn what God wants to teach them.

In his book *Runaway Kids: What Can You Do?* Barry Mishkin says, "Most of today's runaways come home within days or weeks after leaving home. They realized what the outside world was really like and that living their own lives was not the milk and honey existence they thought it was. Shortly after running away from home, their money was gone and they were unable to get a job because of a lack of skills...."[1]

Sound familiar?

The prodigal was a classic example of the runaway in every respect. He came to his senses, not because of his deplorable living conditions but because God brought him to himself. When God wants to get our attention, He knows exactly how to do it!

What's the Big Deal?

What was troubling this prodigal so much? Granted, his father's hired servants had plenty to eat and he did not—but what's the big deal anyway?

Notice first that there were many hired servants, not just one. This may be a clue to the wealth of the prodigal's father. The family farm was so large that many hired servants were needed to work the land. Can't you see the lad pondering how many servants his father had—many, and how few sons—only two? The servants had it better than 50 percent of his father's sons.

Notice as well that the hired servants not only had enough to eat but bread to spare. The verb Jesus used begins with the prefix *peri*, meaning "around." His father's servants were surrounded by loaves of bread. There was more than enough to feed them. There was even enough to feed a prodigal, had he only been there.

And this is what really got to the prodigal. It's subtle, and that's why Jesus included it in His story. These were his father's servants, not his sons or nephews. They were servants, and not even the regular household servants.

In the Ancient Near East, regular workers became part of the extended family. Many served one landowner for life. Hired servants, on the other hand, were day workers. They worked as needed. Landowners would go to the city gate (today it would be the unemployment office) and say, "I need ten men for today. I will pay one silver denarius to each. Who is willing to work?" He would hire them, work them, feed them, pay them, and send them back to the city at night.

Remember Jesus' parable of the day workers in the vineyard (Matt. 20:1-16)? The vineyard owner hired them throughout the day as he needed them. The prodigal remembered that even his father's day workers had a sumptuous lunch each day they worked for him. They had more than they could eat and his father's younger son was starving. Did this make any sense? It makes you wonder.

A Tragic Lesson

There's a lesson here—the lesson of reversed fortunes. Sometimes God allows us to fall into situations that appear to be disastrous. They seem to be the worst possible thing for us.

Our health is reversed. Our finances are reversed. Our spouse moves out of the house. Things are falling apart and we don't understand why. And while there could be a dozen reasons why these things happen, surely one of them is to teach us the blessing of reversed fortunes.

Sometimes the only way God can get our attention is to allow our fortunes to be reversed. When that happens, what do you do? Complain? Get angry with God? Blame Him and become bitter? Or do you look behind your reversed fortunes for God's blessing? Easier said than done, isn't it?

Sometimes God puts us flat on our back in the hospital to get our attention. Sometimes He gets our attention through a rocky marriage. Sometimes our children disappoint us, and through them God gets our attention. But you might as well mark it down: When God wants to get your attention, He will get it! The prodigal was in this pig lot so God could get his attention.

The Tragedy of Inattention

How clearly I remember the first day I saw him. Paul returned to class with his arm in a sling. At first I thought he had just sprained it, but the sling stayed month after month.

As I got to know Paul better, he became more than my student; he became my friend. I learned he had completely lost the use of his arm. It was dead, just lying there limp in that sling. The doctors were hopeful one day he could use it again, but no one knew for sure.

As time went on, Paul faced a decision. He could keep his arm in this lifeless condition, or he could have it removed and be fitted with a prosthesis—an artificial arm. Should he choose the artificial limb, there was no turning back.

Paul agonized over the decision. He sought advice from friends and faculty. Everybody had an opinion. But the decision was his to make. After much prayer, Paul decided to have the immobile arm removed.

In the process of praying for my student friend, he told me what happened to his arm. God had been dealing with Paul about committing his life to the Lord. He thought God may want him to be a youth pastor. But even though he was a Christian and from a fine Christian family, Paul rebelled. He wanted to run his own life. He wanted to make his own decisions. He wanted to choose his own vocation.

Sound familiar?

While running away from God, Paul was involved in a horrible motorcycle accident. He broke his right leg, punctured both lungs and paralyzed his left arm. The guy riding with him wasn't so lucky. He died at the scene of the accident.

My friend lost the use of his arm as a direct result of disobedience to God. God wanted to get his attention, but it took something tragic to get Paul to listen.

While recovering from the accident, Paul's heart began to soften toward God. He yielded himself completely to Christ. Through the advice of godly friends, he decided to come to Bible college to prepare for a lifetime of ministry for the Lord.

I can still see the tears in his eyes and hear the quiver in his voice when Paul said to me, "I paid a terrible price for God to get my attention."

None of us wants to see something like this happen. The prodigal son didn't like feeding the pigs. You don't like having a runaway teen or a prodigal spouse. You don't like the pain they've caused you. But maybe that's just God's way of getting your attention.

If that's true, don't turn away. Don't become bitter. Listen to God's still, small voice. Get His message through the ashes of whatever He is using to get your attention. Surviving the prodigals in your life can bring God's blessing, if you reexamine your relationship with Him.

Beauty From Ashes

By the way, today Paul is serving the Lord as pastor of a local church. He has a wonderful wife and three beautiful daughters and is happy in the Lord. Reversed fortunes can bring good fortunes, if we allow God to speak to us through them.

God used humiliation, hunger and homesickness to get the attention of the prodigal son. What is He using in your life? What's happening to you right now that may be God's way of getting your attention?

Maybe like the prodigal you're running from God. What should you do? Stop, look to God and listen to what He has to say to you. Give Him your undivided attention. Get alone with God in some place of undisturbed solitude.

Block out some time that will be sufficient for you to have a heart-to-heart talk with God. Make it an hour or so. Confess any known sin to Him and then listen.

Quietly wait. Read your Bible and then quietly wait again. Wait for Him to speak to you through what you have read. Let Him have your attention. That's what He really wants. When God gets our attention, He gets the rest of us as well.

Notes

1. Barry D. Mishkin. *Runaway Kids: What Can You Do?* (Dayton, OH: P.P.I. Publishing, 1983), 8.

Chapter 7

HOW TO GO HOME AGAIN

"I gotta go home"

Peggy Walker knows what pain is. She knows what it's like being away from home—a runaway. She's been there. And she knows the relief that comes when you finally stop running and say to yourself, *I gotta go home.*

Peggy was sick a lot as a child. She felt her parents never really wanted her; she knew they didn't love her. They always made her feel their disappointment in her. Peggy was only five when she began to recognize how unhappy she was.

In her early teens she rebelled. She thought her parents were too strict. At age 15 Peggy ran away from home. Like the prodigal in Jesus' family portrait, Peggy went to a city nearly 200 miles away. She wanted nothing to do with her parents. She wanted to be rid of them forever.

In that distant city Peggy found herself alone and on the streets. Looking back now, she deeply regrets getting into drugs and sex and other things too painful to mention. The feeling of failure and disappointment continued to haunt her.

At age 18 Peggy Walker had enough. She was pregnant and wanted to go home. She got into what she terms a "short-term marriage," which only brought continued unhappiness. She never really got things right with her father and mother; the scars in her family remain today.

Peggy says, "I had no idea as a teenager how deeply I hurt my parents. At the time, I didn't care. Now, with a wayward daughter of my own, my hurt is doubled."

It was a long, long way from eating at the bountiful table of the father to slopping the hogs in a foreign land. But the prodigal son traveled that distance in record time.

Destitute and hungry, while all alone in the field, the prodigal came to his senses. He remembered how badly he had treated his father. Accustomed as he was to doing the wrong thing, it was time to do the right thing. The prodigal son resolved to return home and beg for reconciliation with his father.

The moment of truth arrived. In this insightful story Jesus related that the prodigal made this resolve: "I will set out and go back to my father and say to him: Father, I have sinned against heaven and against you. I am no longer worthy to be called your son; make me like one of your hired men" (v. 18).

When prodigals get to this point in their journey, when they make this kind of resolve, they have arrived at the moment of truth. The prodigal son had arrived.

Jesus' Master Plan

That Jesus was the Master Storyteller is evident from this parable. He selected choice words to express the prodigal's resolve. They tell of His five-step master plan for prodigals to receive forgiveness from those they have hurt.

If you're attempting to survive a prodigal in your life, pray that your prodigal will see Jesus' five action steps in this story. If they don't take these steps, they won't come home. These are the steps the Son of God outlines in His story of how a prodigal can come home again.

If you've become alienated from someone, estranged from a person you love, the Savior's five-step master plan is invaluable to you. This is not some clever program to be printed on the back of a card and kept in your purse or wallet. This is the master plan of God, the only plan that works for prodigals of all kinds. This is for you, my friend, if you have wandered into a prodigal lifestyle. This is a way for you to go home again. This is the only way.

All the steps are found in verse 18. They're easy to identify, not so easy to take. If you're ready for your prodigal to come home, or if you're a prodigal and are ready to go home, these may well be the most important pages of this book for you. Get your spiritual sneakers on and let's run through them.

STEP 1—*Personal Determination*

No one has ever been reconciled to a parent, a spouse, a son or a daughter who did not want to be reconciled. You must have a personal determination to be reconciled to someone before you can do anything else. Without it, you won't get to first base.

It's possible the person you've offended doesn't want to be reconciled with you. Maybe that's your dad or mom. Maybe it's a brother or sister. Maybe it's a close friend. Even so, you will never heal the hurt if you lack the personal determination to be reconciled. Don't look to those you've hurt to initiate the process of reconciliation. The first move is always yours. Take responsibility.

Remember the prodigal's first words in the resolve to return to his father: "I will arise." That's personal determination.

In this story the father had no idea where his son was. If there was to be any reconciliation, the son had to make it happen. But the prodigal had come to the end of his rope and wanted to be restored to his father. Like the prodigal, the first move is yours. That's personal determination.

Are you estranged from someone right now? Your estrangement is not just hurting you and the other person; it's also hurting God. I wonder if you have the right stuff to do something about your estrangement? Do you have the personal determination to make the first move?

Please don't misunderstand. If you say you're willing to have a change of mind, it will take courage. The Bible calls that change of mind repentance. If you change your mind about your parents, your son or daughter, your neighbor, your pastor, your ex-husband, you're going to have to call it what God calls it—repentance—and most of us don't like that word. In fact, some like it so little they're willing to be estranged until death just to avoid it.

The first action step in reconciliation is a change of mind that leads to personal determination—"I will arise." If restoration and reconciliation are in your future, they must begin with the personal determination that you will go home again—you must go home again.

STEP 2—*Personal Action*

For most people reconciliation never occurs because they cannot bring themselves to Jesus' first step. But even for some who have a change of mind, reconciliation still does not come. They never put feet to their thoughts. They have personal determination, but they take no personal action.

Not so with the prodigal son. Notice verse 18 says, "I will set out and go back." Those three tiny words "and go back" make all the difference in the world. They spell out the action the son had to take. He couldn't just sit in the corner of a pig lot and change his mind about his father. He had to go home again. He knew personal determination wasn't enough; personal action was also required.

Isn't that true for you as well? If you're looking for reconciliation between your parents and yourself, or your child and yourself, you're going to have to take some personal action. You're going to have to do something about your situation.

One reason we fail to survive the prodigals in our life is because we wait for the other person to make the first move. But the move is yours, Dad and Mom. The move is yours, teenager. If God has brought a change of mind to you about someone, if He has put within your heart the personal determination for reconciliation, it's your move.

Assume the burden of righting the wrong. Never assume the other person will come to you or call you. You must go to them.

Don't think about it. Don't talk about it. Just do it!

It's you God is dealing with; do what He impresses you to do, regardless of how you think your son or daughter will respond. If it's right, do it!

STEP 3—*Personal Confrontation*

The first two steps in reconciliation are easy, compared with the last three. With these steps reconciliation becomes more difficult but also more rewarding.

The prodigal resolved, "I will set out and go back to my father." Remember, these are the words Jesus placed in the mouth of the prodigal. He's the one telling the story. This is what the Savior wants every prodigal to do. It's what He wants you to do if you're estranged from someone you love. Get up and go back, or get up and go after them. Take some action.

Don't miss this; it's too important. The prodigal did not say, "I will set out and go back home." He did not say, "I will arise and return to my native land." He did not simply want to go back home again. His resolve was very specific: "I will set out and go back to my father."

The father was the only one important to the runaway. He wasn't interested in food (though he was hungry). He wasn't interested in friends (though he was lonely). He wasn't interested in new clothes and a warm bed (though he hadn't seen either for a long time). He was only interested in the father.

The prodigal was far from his homeland. He had to have missed it. There's no place like home. He must have yearned for the food that was plentiful at his father's table. Nobody made falafel like his mother. But these things did not lead to his repentance. We do not reconcile with places; we reconcile with people. People are far more significant than places. It was the father he hurt. It was the father he left. It would be to the father he returned.

Real reconciliation requires personal confrontation, eyeball-to-eyeball confrontation. Remember the story of the estranged twin brothers, Jacob and Esau? After being apart for 20 years, Jacob knew he had to return home. But that meant face-to-face contact with his angered brother. It always means that. And let's not pretend that's going to be easy.

But there is no reconciliation without confrontation. If you're to be reconciled with a sister, a mother or a church friend, you must face them squarely and personally, and the sooner the better. Personal confrontation is never easy, but nothing worthwhile ever is.

STEP 4—*Personal Communication*

If facing his father would be hard, imagine what talking to him would be like. The prodigal knew he would have to communicate with his father, communicate personally. He couldn't have someone do it for him. He had to do it himself.

73

"I will arise and go to my father, and will say to him...."

God has given us language to praise Him and to communicate with others. Communication reveals our true feelings, and there's no more direct method of communication than verbal communication.

How many times, husbands, has your wife said to you, "I know you love me, but I'd like to hear you say it once in a while"? Verbal communication is personal communication.

The prodigal knew he had to swallow his pride, return home, meet his father face-to-face, and open his mouth. It was the only way.

It won't be easy for you to speak directly with your parents or your prodigal, but it is necessary. You must go to them. Unless circumstances are impossible, so utterly impossible that you must use the telephone or write a letter, go to them in person. Meet them eyeball-to-eyeball, person to person. Letters and phone calls are weak substitutes for face-to-face communication. And e-mail is the worst form of communication possible when you need to express emotion. Don't resort to electronic reconciliation. Go in person; speak in person.

Pray that God will prepare the way. Ask Him to make your prodigal or parents receptive to you. Check your own heart and motives. Then go. Look them in the eye and open your mouth. Get some communication going.

Remember, when God moves you to reconcile, you don't go alone. He goes with you. God helps open your mouth and He even helps get the words out. Remember Jacob? Before he reconciled with his estranged brother, God promised him, "Go back to your country and your relatives, and I will make you prosper" (Gen. 32:9). Let God prosper you as you are reconciled with those who love you.

STEP 5—*Personal Confession*

Read one last time the words Jesus placed in the mouth of the prodigal. "I will set out and go back to my father and say to him: Father, I have sinned..." (Luke 15:18). Personal determination gave way to personal action. Personal action meant personal confrontation. Personal confrontation required personal communication. And the substance of that personal communication was personal confession.

Some words roll off the tongue so easily. "Hi. How are you?" "Have a good day." "Don't bother to wrap it; I'll take it with me." Other words require significant effort.

"I have sinned." Difficult words to say, aren't they? But restoration requires repentance, and true repentance always requires confession of sin. Saying "I have sinned" and meaning it are the first words in the vocabulary of thanksgiving.

If you really want to be reconciled with your parents, your family or your friends, you need to tell them that you know you've hurt them deeply and you are sorry. You need to convince them, through your presence and your voice, that you feel terrible about what you've done, and in humility you are asking them to forgive you. If they choose not to forgive, that's their business. But you must take care of yours.

Why Go Home Again?

There's one final thing here. If we want to draw all we can from Jesus' parable, we dare not miss this. It's the prodigal's motivation. Why did he resolve to return home? Was it because he was hungry? Because he was dirty? Not at all. He resolved to return because of the hurt he had caused his father.

The prodigal could never get his inheritance back. It was gone forever. He knew that. He had foolishly squandered it.

But he could get his father back, and so can you. You can be restored to your friends or family if you're willing to do what the prodigal did. You can even be restored to your Heavenly Father. But it's a personal thing. It's up to you. You have to want to come home, whether in the physical sense to your family, or in the spiritual sense to God.

Isn't it time you came home again? Isn't it time you came back to the Father, and to the family? If you're restless and have been running from God, remember the words of Augustine, the fourth-century monk and church father. He said to God, "You have made us for Yourself, and the heart of man is restless until it finds rest in You."

There's real hope for every prodigal. There's real hope for you. You can go home again. You can go back to God. You can even go back to your family. Lots of prodigals have. But it's your move.

The Point of No Return

We were rumbling down the runway on a flight from Dallas to Pittsburgh. Suddenly the pilot pulled up and we came to a hard stop. The tower noticed our cargo bay doors were open. Had we taken off, we likely would have had luggage from Texas all the way to Pennsylvania.

For pilots, there's a point of no return. It's the point at which they can't pull up and they must become airborne. We hadn't reached that point. We could go back to the terminal, back home again.

Perhaps you're estranged from someone you love. Maybe you've convinced yourself you can't go home again. You think you've gone too far and you can't go back. What you said or did was just too embarrassing. The hurt can never be undone.

The prodigal must have felt like that, too, but he was wrong. It is possible to go home again. There's someone there waiting for you. You haven't reached the point of no return, but you've probably reached the point you should return! Like our pilot, you can pull up and go home again.

Whether you've run away from home, left your spouse, or harbor hard feelings toward someone in your family or church, Jesus' five-step plan for reconciliation is the only hope you have. But it is hope, real hope. It can be real for you, if you want it to be. The decision is yours.

Going home again is an act of the will—your will. Follow Jesus' five-step master plan for reconciliation. You can go home again. You must go home again.

PRODIGALS IN CHRISTIAN FAMILIES

Bill and Carole Frasier

Bill and Carole Frasier were both raised in Christian homes. Their parents were devout, diligent and loving, but strict. Neither Bill nor Carole ever seriously entertained the idea of going against their parents. It wasn't natural; it wasn't what Christian kids did. So when Bill and Carole were married and began their own family, raising them in a devout, diligent and loving, but strict home, they naturally assumed their children would be just as they were. So much for assumptions.

The Frasiers have three children. Their first was a girl, whom they loved dearly. They named her Tammy. Carole was especially happy to have a daughter in whom she could invest her life. Then God gave them two sons. The oldest was William Jr.; they just called him Will. Four years later their youngest was born. Bill wanted to call him *Caboose* because "he was the end of the line," but cooler heads prevailed and they named him Chad.

Life was good for the Frasier family. Bill had a job in Silicon Valley and Carole was a full-time mother. But they were not the typical nuclear family. They were always there for their kids. They took time with them, did "dad and mom" things with them. It was a happy family.

Each of the Frasier children trusted Christ as Savior at an early age. Each showed all the signs of following in the Lord's will. But that was when they were kids. When kids become teens, sometimes they undergo incredible spiritual and social upheavals, and that's what happened to Tammy.

Going Underground

In Bill's own words, "Something changed in middle adolescence.

I don't know for sure what it was to this day. But Tammy began to do things never done by anyone in our extended families. She went 'underground' with her life. She began to deceive us and resist us in a passive-aggressive pattern."

When Tammy was a sophomore in high school, she began to skip classes and run around with friends who, while they claimed to be Christians, had very unchristian habits and attitudes. They were rebels at heart. Tammy liked to stay out late, as most high school teens do, but she would regularly violate her curfew and then dispute with her parents why she even needed a curfew. Academically Tammy was on the skids at school. She dropped from being an honor roll student to barely passing. Clearly something was wrong.

Carole confides, "I always wanted to be a wife and mother. That was to be my only career. The births of my children were the high points of my life. Every stage of growth brought new delights and new challenges. I was prepared for them all. I did my homework. But absolutely nothing prepared me for a rebellious teenager."

Bill was a respected leader in their local church. Both he and Carole did some lay counseling as a part of the church's ministry. God had used them to help others through difficult times, and they were sure God would use them with Tammy too. So backed by Carole, Bill began to challenge his daughter to get her act together and quit goofing off. He wanted her to get more serious about school. In fact, Bill gave Tammy both an ultimatum and an alternative. She could either clean up her act at school or they would take her out of the public school altogether.

Slipping Away

The Frasiers were desperate. They always believed that if you did certain things in raising your kids, they had to turn out all right. It was a simple formula like $2 + 2 = 4$. But Tammy was slipping further and further away from them, and they knew it. Something had to be done, even something as drastic as removing her from her school friends. Bill says, "I'll never forget the night we broke the news to her. Tammy was very unhappy with our decision. We could barely cope with her and she fought everything we tried to do. Eventually, we decided that if she was going to goof off in high school, we would home school her instead. This would give her the opportunity to get a job and learn some responsibility, and give us the chance to monitor her progress. That seemed the best plan."

Tammy got a job at the local pizza place. Bill and Carole thought things would get better. They didn't. Tammy was a very attractive girl and she had always used her beauty to win friends and influence people. Tammy's boss, contrary to company policy, took a romantic interest in her. She was just 17; he was seven years older.

The Frasiers were concerned about Tammy's innocence as well as the age difference and character of her boss. He was anything but the "boyfriend of their dreams." You know those commercials where the scrubby, undesirable boyfriend comes to the door to pick up the daughter? That was this guy. Bill especially didn't like his looks. "What kind of guy wears an earring and looks like that?"

A New Boyfriend

Tammy's boyfriend/boss made no profession of knowing the Lord as Savior, and that worried Bill and Carole more than anything. They explained to Tammy why this wasn't a good idea. She didn't care. Finally they put their foot down. Tammy wasn't to see him again. Somehow they knew that wasn't going to work.

Worried, occasionally Bill and Carole would go looking for Tammy in the city late at night and find them together. However, when Tammy came home well past curfew, she simply refused to talk about it. The Frasiers not only disciplined her appropriately but prayed earnestly that somehow, something would happen to turn Tammy around, but to no avail.

At their wits' end, Bill and Carole sought the advice of their pastor, who was a lifelong friend of the family. The pastor saw the three of them several times. Carole worked with Tammy and helped her get her GED certificate and graduate. They thought with an accomplishment like that, maybe throwing a party would help Tammy come around. They gave her a party to remember. But instead of being thankful, Tammy wanted more liberal rules now that she was 18. The Frasiers bent some to try to accommodate their only daughter, but it finally got to the point that their pastor agreed they had to draw a firm line to put an end to the constant tension.

"That was the hardest day of my life," Bill recalls. "We told

Tammy, 'Either live with our rules or leave our house and make your own.' It didn't take long for her to decide. Tammy packed her things and moved out."

Tammy's departure meant parental pain for Bill and Carole. They rarely saw their daughter or even heard from her. They did hear about her occasionally from other people, but all they heard were the rumors of her wild lifestyle. She even secretly became engaged to Jason, the man Bill and Carole had forbidden her to see.

Wedding Bells

In the spring of 1996, Tammy called her mom and dad and said Jason and she wanted to talk. The Frasiers knew instinctively what they wanted, and Carole began having panic attacks due to the stress she was under. "We met at a local restaurant," Carole remembers, "since Jason wouldn't set foot in our house."

To the Frasier's surprise, Tammy and Jason wanted to tell them that they had gone about this relationship all wrong. They admitted that they lied to her mom and dad, but wanted their blessing to get married. Bill and Carole were skeptical, as any parent would be, and thought their "out" was to suggest that they wait six months and have proper premarital counseling done by the pastor. They knew this counseling would include a spiritual inventory and confrontation with the Gospel.

Both Jason and Tammy agreed. In the counseling sessions Jason gave all the right answers, so the Frasiers yielded and moved from adversaries to advocates. They gave Tammy the wedding of her dreams. Carole confides, "Our hearts weren't in it, but we accepted Jason and worked on it even though he was reluctant to meet us halfway."

Double Jeopardy

Bill and Carole's suspicions were well-founded. A year into their marriage Jason was unfaithful to Tammy, and they never recovered. However, she was not without her share of the responsibility. Before they were divorced, Tammy began living with the husband of the woman with whom Jason had been unfaithful. It was a more twisted plot than any soap opera.

The Frasiers were shattered and pled with Tammy to come to her senses and consider the "double-jeopardy" she had placed herself in. To no avail. She wanted to marry this man, whose name was Brett. In fact, she wanted her parents to meet him. He, too, was not a believer in the Lord, so Bill and Carole begged Tammy to move back home until they were married, but she would not.

"Oddly enough, it was Brett in whom we first saw light at the end of the tunnel. He was seeking God and under great conviction from the Lord. So he began to attend church with us." Bill met Brett for lunch one day so they could get to know one another better. They also talked about their situation and Tammy's past. It was a positive and honest experience, and Brett began to understand why Bill wouldn't bless their marriage plans. Brett promised that Tammy and he would not marry unless she first reconciled with her parents. He stuck to his promise, as did Tammy.

Big Breakthroughs

One Sunday after church, Brett sought out the pastor and set an appointment to meet him the following day. Brett was ready to make some life changes. The Spirit of God was wooing him, drawing him to the Savior. The pastor led Brett to the Lord that day. It was almost too good to be true for Bill and Carole.

At about the same time, Tammy came to see Bill and Carole, wanting to reconnect with her family. Her two brothers were more angry with her than anyone realized. Their sister disappointed them, alienated herself from the family and caused untold anxiety and plenty of tears. But God was in it all, and even the boys showed a willingness to forgive Tammy and reconcile the Frasier family differences.

As a family they began to meet every Tuesday night for three months. These were family-only affairs. They would vent their anger, express their disappointments and give reasons why they thought there was such a family meltdown. Bill recalls, "It was very painful for all of us. But it helped us empty our emotional tanks and move toward forgiveness and acceptance as we all spoke our piece."

Doing the Right Thing

But there was still the issue of Tammy and Brett living together.

That was something the Frasiers couldn't condone. One night they went over to the apartment where Brett and Tammy were living, to confront them on this issue. Much to Bill and Carole's surprise, both Brett and Tammy understood. In fact, they already had decided if they were to get things right with the Lord and with her parents, they needed to stop living together. Tammy stayed in the apartment and Brett went back to live with his parents until things were made right.

God was doing a work of His grace in the hearts of Brett and Tammy. In fact, He was doing a work of grace in the hearts of the whole Frasier family. In December 1999, with the blessing of Mom, Dad and two brothers, Brett and Tammy were united in marriage.

Bill says, "Since then I have been involved in weekly discipleship time with Brett to help him get up to speed on the key doctrines and issues of the Bible. It has been a wonderful experience for both of us."

On the Way Back

The Frasiers have seen growth, healing and love return to their home. Brett and Tammy come over two or three times each week to enjoy what they had been missing. It was like the prodigal son in Jesus' parable. Once home, he began to enjoy all that he missed through his own foolishness. Now the Frasiers spend every Sunday together, first in church, then out for dinner, and then back to the house to do all the things families were meant to enjoy.

So are things back where they were before their family nightmare began? "Not entirely," Bill says. "It's not an overnight thing. It takes time. Tammy isn't all the way there just yet, and there is need for spiritual growth and honest acknowledgment of past mistakes, but that will come. We've come such a long way as a family already. We've all learned so much."

The Frasiers acknowledge that God is good and that restoration and forgiveness are powerful gifts from God. They have their daughter back. They are growing together as a family, and even though they still see room for improvement, they are a family again. They know from experience that it's God's grace that heals wounds and binds people together in spite of past hurts.

Lessons Learned

Did the experience of having a prodigal daughter teach the Frasiers anything about life, about themselves, about God? Lots of things. "For one," Carole said, "I learned that some things can only be experienced through pain and suffering. It's not because we deserved the pain or did something wrong. And it's not because we were not walking close to the Lord. We were. But sometimes there is no other way."

"And another thing we discovered," says Carole, "was that the Bible is filled with prodigals. They are a part of God's plan, and prodigalism is not an unusual thing to God. He has a plan for prodigals just like He has a plan for the rest of us. We simply have to learn what that plan is and trust His timing to bring it to His conclusion."

The Frasiers also have come to some conclusions about forgiveness. Forgiveness is the only answer to a deeply wounded soul. "Forgiveness doesn't mean that what Tammy did was right, but it releases Bill and me from the anger and bitterness that seeped into our souls because of how Tammy hurt us," Carole concluded.

Bill and Carole have deepened their trust in the Lord through their prodigal wars. Proverbs 3:5-6 has become their constant companion. They no longer feel like failures as parents, not so much because Tammy came back to them but because they realize that they did the right thing. The right thing in God's hands is always success.

Part Two

THE STAY-AT-HOME KID
When Prodigals Stay at Home and You Wish They'd Run Away

Chapter 8

THE OTHER PRODIGAL

"The Crabgrass Kid"

I love coffee. When I first started drinking coffee (in college—where else?), I savored the aroma and endured the taste. Now, with the advent of gourmet coffees, even the taste is something to write home about. Hazelnut and French Vanilla are my favorites.

Everyone talks about how good coffee smells. Why doesn't someone make an air freshener with the scent of brewed coffee? The aroma is so inviting. We breathe deeply. The sight of steam rising from the cup draws us to it like moths to a flame.

The taste is rich and full. But when we are finished drinking, we see them. Grounds. Ugly, gritty grounds in the bottom of our cup. Surprise, surprise.

If Jesus' parable of the prodigal son were a cup of coffee, we now have come to the grounds—the older brother. As Jesus told His parable, it became painfully evident there were two prodigals in this story. One left home, the other didn't.

This is a story about interpersonal relationships between a father and his two disappointing sons. Jesus did not tell this parable because He liked to tell stories. The Master Storyteller had a specific audience hanging on every word—the Pharisees and scribes (Luke 15:2-3).

In many respects, you don't get to the prodigal son until you get to the older brother. He may not be the most interesting character, but he certainly is the point of the parable.

Surviving the prodigals in your life begins with observation. If you cannot identify prodigal behavior in those around you, you cannot help them, let alone survive them. Chief among the obstacles to surviving a prodigal is our failure to see them as prodigals.

Before we identify the feelings and emotions of the father sandwiched between these two sons, let's get inside the head of the older brother and see how he responded to his sibling's return.

Another Prodigal Son

Here's how Jesus painted this family. The father was gentle, fair and kind, and was crunched between two sons. The younger son was impetuous, self-centered and arrogant, and was now a whipped puppy. The older brother? He's a case study in self-righteousness, a withered branch on the family tree.

Someone has said that older brothers are the crabgrass on the lawn of life. I have an older brother, and I've always told him that was true. But the older brother in Jesus' story was the crabgrass kid. He needed a good dose of herbicide, as did the Pharisees and scribes whom he represented.

Read what Jesus said: "Meanwhile, the older son was in the field. When he came near the house, he heard music and dancing. So he called one of the servants and asked him what was going on. 'Your brother has come,' he replied, 'and your father has killed the fattened calf because he has him back safe and sound'" (Luke 15:25-27).

The day the younger son demanded his inheritance was a turning point in the lives of each family member. For the prodigal, the decision was easy. He would journey to a far country in search of his freedom. It's what he wanted more than anything in life.

But the older brother had a decision to make as well. He, too, received his inheritance that day. He could join his impetuous sibling on the Mad Hatter's escapade, or he could stay home and work for the father. The older brother decided to stay by the stuff. He would work hard and do the right thing.

While the younger prodigal was gallivanting around the world, the older brother remained faithful. He never left his father's home. He did his job day in and day out. He was a model son, the epitome of faithfulness.

The older brother possessed many commendable qualities, but he was still a prodigal. He was guilty of at least two things.

First, he was guilty of surprise when the prodigal son returned.

And second, he was guilty of anger when he would not join the celebration for his wayward brother. We'll think about his anger in the next chapter. Let's concentrate on the sin of surprise.

Strange Twists to the Story

Absorbed in himself and his work, the older brother became quite accustomed to the prodigal being gone. He was in the field the day his brother came home. When he came in from the field, the older prodigal heard music and dancing. He didn't have a clue what was going on.

I find that odd, don't you? After all, there were only two sons in this family. When the prodigal returned, don't you think it's strange that no one bothered to rush the news to the older brother? No one took the time to tell him. He discovered the happy news only when he came in from working the fields, presumably at the end of the day.

And here's something even stranger. The servants knew everything—knew the whole story—and they were the ones who finally told the older brother.

Maybe it went like this. The son came near enough to the house to hear the music. He inquired, "Hey, what's happening? What's all the noise?" The servants responded, "Oh, haven't you heard?" "Heard what?" the older son responded. "He's back! Your brother has come home again. We thought you knew."

How embarrassing, being the last to know! It's like being the last kid picked for the team in gym class. He must have felt like a fool.

But the older brother was not kept in the dark intentionally. Likely the father and servants were caught up in the moment, so taken back by the prodigal's sudden appearance they simply assumed someone had told the older brother. That could easily have happened. Certainly a compassionate father would not purposefully keep such happy news from a son he loved.

Left Behind

The box office hit movie *Home Alone* illustrates this perfectly. It's the story of a family who went on vacation; and in all the flurry of activity before their flight, they inadvertently left their precocious youngest son home alone.

The older brother may well have felt like this little boy. No one seemed to care for him. No one showed him any concern. No one bothered to get him when they left for the airport. And no one went into the fields to tell the older brother the prodigal had returned.

Maybe you've felt like that. You've been faithful in your local church. Everything you were asked to do, you did. When the burden of added responsibility was placed on your shoulders, no one seemed to notice. No one ever said thanks. No one cared.

Then, suddenly, someone who had wandered away from the life of your church returned and all eyes were focused on him or her. That prodigal got all the attention, and you got none. You were surprised when they returned, and not a little angered. You must have felt like the older brother in Jesus' story. How would you ever survive this prodigal reentering the life of your church?

But remember, the older brother is also a prodigal son in this parable. If we're to survive the prodigals in our lives, the first thing we must do is make sure we're not one of them.

The Sound of Music

The prodigal's return took the older brother by surprise. Jesus said, "When he came near the house, he heard music and dancing."

The word Jesus chose for music certainly doesn't imply a simple celebration. We get our English word "symphony" from it. It's the Greek word *symphonias*, meaning the harmony created by a band of musicians.

When the prodigal came home, the father didn't sing a joyful ditty. And this wasn't the music of the servants or other banqueters. This may imply professional music, performed by entertainers. Sufficient time had elapsed for an orchestra to be hired and for serious celebrating to begin.

What do you suppose went through the older prodigal's mind? The older brother was completely in the dark. He had no idea what was going on. He was taken by surprise at the prodigal's return. But that was his error. He was surprised when the prodigal came home. The older brother was guilty of the sin of surprise.

Overtaken by Surprise

Think about it. Was the father surprised when the prodigal came home again? Not at all. Why? I think the day his son left home the father began praying God would bring him back. When the prodigal finally came home again, it was no surprise.

But what about the older brother? Had he prayed for the prodigal's return? Apparently not. He had no idea what this celebration was all about. He wasn't expecting his brother to come home again and was guilty of surprise when he did.

The older prodigal convinced himself that his brother was gone forever. He likely said good riddance to him for bringing shame to the family name. No wonder he had to ask the servants what was happening when he came in from the field. He was overtaken by surprise.

Jesus included the crabgrass kid in His story to turn the spotlight on the Pharisees and scribes. They were the older brothers of Israel. They were surprised to see Jesus eating with sinners and treating them with the kindness of the father in this story. He told it for their benefit. But for the 21st-century church, there's a pointed application.

Reclaimed Backsliders

Many in the church today are just as surprised as the older brother when a prodigal comes back to the Lord. For some it's because they never prayed for that young couple who left the church. Others never have been ashamed of the way they treated that single parent who stopped coming because she was not made to feel welcome.

It's no wonder we are surprised when church prodigals return. We never have made any effort to bring them back into the life of the family.

There are some folks in church today who are the epitome of faithfulness, just like this older brother. Unlike the father, however, they never ask God to bring a prodigal home again to the church family. They never scan the horizon for them. They simply write them off and make no attempt to recover them. If prodigal parishioners return, these faithful members will surely be surprised.

It's a horrible thing to be surprised when God does what He has promised to do. God is in the business of reclaiming backsliders, just as He is in the business of saving sinners. And if God gets ahold of someone who has wandered away from the family, we should not be surprised. That's what God's grace is all about. Why should we be surprised when God does what He is in the business of doing?

Rooting Out Surprise

Like the older brother, if we haven't asked God to perform a work of grace in prodigal hearts, we'll be surprised when they return. Our kids will come back home and we'll be so shocked we won't know what to say. Like the older brother, if we haven't cared enough to pray that young couple back to church, we'll be surprised speechless when they return.

It's a sad thing to be surprised when God does His work in a prodigal's heart. But when the prodigal son came home again, the crabgrass kid was guilty of surprise, and that was sin. It reflected a lack of faith in God's ability to reclaim what was lost.

Do you know someone who has become a prodigal? Maybe none of your children were prodigals, but what about someone who has wandered away from the life of your church? Some family who used to attend, but now are living far from God? If so, just because they live the life of a prodigal doesn't mean you should live the life of an older brother.

Pray for that person or family. Ask God specifically to touch them, to convict them of their sin, to bring them to themselves and to draw them back where they belong, back home again. Do whatever you can to attract them back to the life of the family. And when God does His marvelous work of grace in their hearts, don't be surprised. Be a survivor. But don't be a surprised survivor.

God's Business

Ask someone what business they're in and they'll say, "Me? I'm a craftsman. I fashion beautiful things with my hands." "Oh, I'm a corporate executive. I run a large company." "My business? I'm a physician. I heal people." "I'm proud to say I'm a homemaker. I love and care for my family."

Do you know what business God is in? He's a craftsman—the Creator of all things. He's an executive—the Sovereign of the universe. He's the ultimate healer—the Great Physician. He's the family caregiver—caring for all His children. But God is also in the reclamation business. He reclaims those who have stumbled onto the junk pile of life.

God's business is providing real hope to hopeless people. Don't be surprised when He brings your runaway home. Don't be surprised when He brings your prodigal spouse home again. And don't be surprised when that church member who hasn't been in church for years returns. That's God's business too. He reclaims people— prodigal people—and He can reclaim your prodigal, if you ask Him.

If you're waiting for someone to come home again, don't spoil their return with surprise. Don't be like the crabgrass kid. Let God be about His business.

Chapter 9

WHEN BROTHERS HATE BROTHERS

"Conquered by anger"

The older brother's sin of surprise was a passive sin. Surprise, more or less, overtook him. It wasn't something he expected. By definition, a surprise is not something for which you plan. It came as a result of a lack in his life—a lack of concern, compassion and care for his younger brother. This was the same kind of lack Jesus found in the Pharisees and scribes.

But surprise was not the older prodigal's only sin; and his second sin was not passive but incredibly active. Much more deadly than surprise, the older brother was also guilty of anger.

Here's what Jesus said in verses 25-28. "Meanwhile, the older son was in the field. When he came near the house, he heard music and dancing. So he called one of the servants and asked him what was going on. 'Your brother has come,' he replied, 'and your father has killed the fattened calf because he has him back safe and sound.' The older brother became angry and refused to go in. So his father went out and pleaded with him."

Inappropriate Anger

The older brother was guilty of the double sins of surprise and anger. Of the two, anger was the more serious.

So angry was he, both at his brother for returning home and at his father for welcoming him back, that this older brother refused to enter the house. He was angry, and he wanted everyone to know it.

Do you think anger is sin? Doesn't the Bible say it's okay to be angry? In fact it does. In Psalm 4:4 David says, "In your anger do not sin; when you are on your beds, search your hearts and be silent." Paul quotes David in Ephesians 4:26, "'In your anger do not sin': Do not let the sun go down while you are still angry."

There it is in black and white. The older brother had every right to get angry. But if you're looking to Psalm 4:4 or Ephesians 4:26 to justify the older brother's anger, look again. These verses do not say it is always right to get angry.

Ephesians 4:26 says we can be angry, but just five verses later Paul says, "Get rid of all bitterness, rage and anger, brawling and slander, along with every form of malice."

Can we reconcile these verses? Is it acceptable to get angry? Yes. In fact, on some occasions, it's necessary. Even God got angry (see 1 Kings 11:9; 2 Kings 17:18; Ps. 7:11; 79:5; Heb. 12:29). The psalmist Asaph begs, "O LORD God Almighty, how long will your anger smolder against the prayers of your people?" (Ps. 80:4).

We know the Lord Jesus got angry (Mark 3:5). John 2:13-17 records Him making a whip of cords and angrily driving a bunch of profiteering pirates out of the temple at Passover.

When Is Anger Appropriate?

Anger can be appropriate, but the keys to appropriate anger are context, motivation and object. Are we angry in the right place, for the right reason, at the right thing? We must always filter our anger through these questions.

For example, Moses became angry on several occasions. Sometimes his anger was justified; other times not. Sometimes God condoned his anger; other times He condemned it.

When Moses came down from Mount Sinai and found the Israelites worshiping the golden calf, he threw the two tablets of stone to the ground, smashing them in anger. But that anger was righteous indignation, justifiable anger over the sin of God's people. Remember, in the same chapter (Ex. 32) God was angry at Israel for exactly the same reason (vv. 10,12).

Later Moses became angry when the Israelites once again complained because they had no water to drink (Num. 20:4-5). God told him to take his rod, stand on a nearby rock and speak to the rock.

Water would pour out of it. Sounds simple enough. Moses would demonstrate God's power and his faith in God at the same time.

Instead, exasperated by the continual complaints of the people, Moses struck the rock twice and said, "Must we bring you water out of this rock?" (Num. 20:10). God had told him to bring water out of the rock, but not that way. Moses' theatrics, his lack of faith, and his claim that this was something Aaron and he must do instead of Jehovah, earned God's displeasure.

The anger of the older brother in Jesus' parable fell into this latter category. His anger clearly was not righteous indignation. The older brother thought himself to be righteous, but he was only self-righteous. He was not angry at his brother's sin—and this is the key—he was angry at his father's compassion. The object of his anger was wrong. He was guilty of inappropriate anger.

Airline Anger Anecdote

I was checking in at the United Airlines counter in Honolulu when I heard a young prima donna behind me. "I don't carry my bag. Someone else carries my bag."

His accent was British but a bit fake. He was young, perhaps 25 or 26. It was evident he thought he was somebody. I have no idea who he was, but he certainly was causing a commotion.

Airline personnel had asked him to take his bag from a pre-check-in counter to the check-in counter, but he refused. He left it in the middle of the floor. The woman behind the counter said she would have to call security and report an unattended bag if he didn't pick it up and bring it to her.

The peacock got angry. "I'll sue this airline for breach of service [whatever that is]. I'll not be treated this way. I expect service." He rambled on at the top of his lungs for a few more minutes. We all stood by snickering. When he discerned that no one was going to serve him as he demanded, he finally gave in, picked up his bag and grumbled over to the counter.

Inappropriate anger. Occasionally we're all afflicted by it. But we must never confuse Ephesians 4:26 with this kind of anger. The older prodigal's anger was not righteous anger; it was sin.

An Explosion of Anger

When the crabgrass kid saw his father had welcomed the prodigal home, when he saw that his father gave a celebration for the prodigal and that no such celebration had ever been given for him, this older son exploded with anger.

I say "exploded" because that's what Jesus said. The older brother blew up in a rage. He was not mildly miffed; he exploded.

The word Jesus used for "anger" is *orge*. It means "wrath," a much more stringent emotion than anger. This word betrays the older prodigal's long-standing resentment toward his wayward brother. It had been boiling for years, simmering just beneath the surface. The whole time the younger son was out living it up, the older brother was at home in the fields being eaten alive with anger.

Ralph Waldo Emerson said, "For every minute you are angry, you lose 60 seconds of happiness." This older son was losing a lifetime.

The older brother was the faithful son. That's commendable. But his faithfulness served only as a mask for his resentment. Inside he was bitter and resentful toward his brother. And now he became bitter toward his father for taking this wretched sinner back into the family. He was especially bitter because the father took the prodigal back with no little fanfare. The brother's resentment erupted like the hot steam of a geyser.

The Anesthetic of the Mind

The sin of surprise has now been supplanted by the sin of anger, and the fruit of anger is seen in the words "and refused to go in."

"No sir, I'm not going in there. Not as long as that sinner is in there. What fellowship has light with darkness? I can't go in there. I refuse. I'm not going to join the celebration. I hate my brother—my father too—for showing kindness to him. I'll never go in that house again." Can't you just hear the older brother?

It's the self-righteous rationalization of a Pharisee. The older brother wasn't thinking straight. Would he allow his anger to exclude him from all the benefits of the family? Yes, he would. C. S. Lewis called anger the anesthetic of the mind, and this older brother proved you cannot be reasonable and angry at the same time.

The crabgrass kid hated his younger brother so much that when the prodigal got right with the father, this brother wouldn't give him the opportunity to get right with him.

Anger in the Church

You've seen this attitude in your church, haven't you? There are some church members who, when a prodigal comes back to the life of the church family, are not only surprised but angry.

"I'm not going to that church ever again. They open their arms to people who have sinned, and they welcome them back just because they've repented of their sin. Why, the first thing you know that prodigal will park in my parking place. He'll sit in my favorite pew. Before long, he'll want to teach my Bible study group. Nope, I'm not going in there."

But the older brother was wrong, and so are church members who act like him. Certainly the prodigal wandered away from the life of the family. Certainly he lived wickedly in the world. Certainly he brought shame to the father and to the family name. But the Spirit of God convicted him and brought him back to the father. He genuinely repented of his sin, returned to his father and sought restoration.

While the father joyously received him, the older brother jealously rejected him.

What about you? As a faithful church member have you been acting like the older brother in Jesus' parable? Are you learning how to survive the prodigals in your church, or are you so angry that you reject them?

If you've detected a bit of the older brother in your life recently, take off the clothes of self-righteousness and the glasses of self-deceit and see yourself as God sees you—bitter, resentful, jealous, unforgiving. In short, see yourself as the prodigal that stayed home and sinned against the prodigal that wandered away. Prodigals come in all shapes and sizes. Some of them are even in the church.

Hard Questions

If God has gotten hold of a prodigal and brought him or her back to your church family, are you taking a "wait and see" attitude? Do you want to see if their repentance is genuine before you welcome them back? If so, ask yourself these questions: "Is this what the father did in Jesus' parable? Did he wait for his son to return? Did he send him into the field for a trial period to see if his repentance was real?" You know the answers.

Those same questions apply to your family. One of your children becomes a prodigal, slams the door behind her and stomps out of your life. Now your daughter wants to come back. What "wait and see" attitudes will you adopt, Dad? Do you set up conditions for your daughter's return? Did the father in Jesus' parable? We'll look more specifically at this in a later chapter, but you know what the answer is. The father knew God had answered his prayers. He knew his son had returned broken and selfless. He was not only willing but eager to accept him back.

One of the hardest things for us to admit as Christians is that we have been an older brother. It's much easier to admit we've been a prodigal. But if we know our attitudes and actions toward others in our home family or church family are not pleasing to our Heavenly Father, there's only one thing for us to do. We must do what the younger prodigal did. We must repent of our sin—the sin of jealousy, resentment and anger. We must return to our Father for restoration and fellowship. Even though we've never left home, we must be willing to come home again. And we must reconcile with those we've sinned against.

Anger is acid, an insidious acid. It does more damage to the container it's stored in than to anything it's poured on. It eats through the lining of the heart and sours the spirit. It's one of Satan's strongest weapons. With anger he can blind our eyes to the obvious, plug our ears to the evident, close our minds to the logical. If a prodigal returns and you persist in your anger, you are the ultimate loser. That's why the Scriptures beg us to deal with our anger on a daily basis.

When anger erupts, provide for its controlled ventilation. Avoid either extreme—blowing up or keeping it in. With the first you lose another; with the second you lose yourself. Either way, you'll pay a heavy price if you allow yourself to be conquered by anger.

Chapter 10

WHAT'S EATING THE OLDER BROTHER?

"Poor old me"

The heart is an incredible organ. In a normal person, the heart beats 70 times a minute, 100,000 times a day, 40 million times a year! It takes a strong muscle to pump 11,000 quarts of blood a day, 265 million quarts in an average lifetime. Yet as strong as the heart is, nothing hurts more than a hurting heart.

The older brother in Jesus' family portrait was eaten up with anger. He was hurting inside and no one knew. Suddenly it all came spilling out in his anguished words to the father.

Have you noticed how sometimes we hide our feelings with words? Words are supposed to reveal feelings, to convey ideas. But frequently the words we choose hide as much as they reveal. The older brother's words both hid and revealed his inner feelings. Here's his complaint.

"Look! All these years I've been slaving for you and never disobeyed your orders. Yet you never gave me even a young goat so I could celebrate with my friends. But when this son of yours who has squandered your property with prostitutes comes home, you kill the fattened calf for him!" (Luke 15:29-30).

The Psychology of Self-Pity

Pretty vengeful words, aren't they? They clearly display a hurting heart. They also betray the bruised psyche of self-pity.

There is a certain psychology to self-pity. When someone feels they have been forgotten or emotionally abused, they hurt deep inside. And when those hurt feelings erupt, they remarkably parallel the words of the older brother.

Do you think the older brother was used to speaking harshly to his father? I don't. Likely he had never talked back to his father. He claimed he had never broken any of his father's commandments, and in a Jewish home surely that would have included respect for his father. Still, when the younger son returned, the older brother erupted like a volcano and spewed out his bitter ash all over his father.

How could this have happened? What circumstances led to such a bitter confrontation? What was in the older brother's heart when he blew up at his father? Let's take a closer look at the psychology of self-pity.

Misperceived Relationships

The older brother was hurt by his misperceived relationship with his father. He blurted out, "Look! All these years I've been slaving for you."

Sounds harmless enough. The older brother was reminding his father that while the younger son was out gallivanting around the world, he had remained faithful. But there was a serious flaw in the way he perceived his relationship to the father. The father viewed his son one way; the son viewed his father another. That led to years of hurt and misunderstanding.

What was his misconception? The crabgrass kid used the verb for *slaving*, not *serving*, when he described his relationship with his father. That's huge. It is the kind of thing a psychologist is looking for in a conversation with his patient. The older brother viewed himself in virtual slavery to his father.

There. It was out! The pain in his heart was finally expressed. His hurt took words. While his father viewed their relationship as father and son, the older brother viewed that relationship as master and slave.

All these years the older prodigal secretly despised his father as a slave despises his master. His mind had been playing games with him since his youth. Years of repressed hurt spilled out in a single sentence.

Instead of enjoying a family relationship, the older brother's misconception produced only a work relationship with his father. He never enjoyed the benefits of being a son because he always viewed his father as someone to be served, not someone to be loved.

Indentured Servants

Unfortunately, many sons and daughters in Christian homes today have the same misconception. Maybe it's happened in your home. Those little jobs around the house, those chores around the barn, are not viewed as the responsibilities of a family working together, but rather as a violation of personal rights.

Recently I was in a Christian home in another country. Being the guest in the home for a week allowed me opportunity to observe the dynamics of the home. The father failed to take his responsibility to be the leader in his home. His business consumed all his time. The mother was left with the full responsibility of raising the children. While the kids were well-mannered and polite, when the mother would ask for them to do a simple chore like the dishes or making a bed, the response from her children was always simply disobedient silence. They saw helping out around the home as indentured servitude.

It's good for your children to have responsibilities around the house. It helps them develop maturity, responsibility and gratitude. Besides, that's the payment they pay for the space they rent in your family.

During their growing-up years my children had personal responsibilities (like cleaning their own room) and family responsibilities (like washing dishes, feeding the dog, etc.). There was a division of labor, and Mom and Dad had responsibilities too. But you only survive the prodigals in your life if your kids' attitude toward these responsibilities is reasonable service and not forced slavery.

Some teenagers have badly misconceived their relationship to the family. They see themselves only as indentured servants. If you're to survive the prodigals in your life, you have to talk with your children about their feelings. Give them reasons why everybody in the family participates in the chores. And make sure that Dad and Mom are doers of the work, not just delegators.

His misconceived relationship with the father caused the older brother incredible hurt. But the psychology of self-pity goes deeper than that.

Heartless Obedience

The older brother's psyche was also hurt by heartless obedience. On the heels of his sad comment about slaving for his father is the equally sad comment about never disobeying his father's orders.

At first glance this, too, may appear to be a positive declaration. But it reflects the meaninglessness of his submission to the father. The older brother gave only heartless obedience. Self-pity was born from submission without joy.

It's precisely here that Jesus drove home His point to the Pharisees and scribes. They were older brothers, for they viewed their relationship with God as slavish bondage instead of spontaneous freedom. The older son said he had never transgressed his father's commands. The Pharisees believed they had never transgressed the Law. They were convinced that every statute, every precept, every interpretation of the rabbis had been kept. And if they did transgress the Law, their scholars devised innumerable ways to interpret the Law so they would appear to be innocent.

Paul said he was like that as a Pharisee. Recounting the pride he had in his ancestral pedigree, he said that as far as legalistic righteousness was concerned, he was faultless (Phil. 3:6). As a Jew, Saul of Tarsus fulfilled all the statutes, precepts and principles required by the Law. He was without blame. But when he was subdued by Christ as Savior and Lord, God declared Paul to be righteous in Jesus Christ, and being declared righteous is better than being convinced you are blameless any day!

The older brother had hurt for years because he gave meaningless obedience to his father. He never obeyed out of love for his father. He only obeyed out of duty.

Is it that way with you? Do you obey the commands of your Heavenly Father out of duty alone? Are you faithful in attending church because you love the Father and His family, or are you afraid of what others will think if you don't attend? If we obey out of duty, fear or self-righteousness, we are miserable sons indeed.

Heartless obedience is not obedience at all. Obedience is doing what we're told to do, when we're told to do it, with the right heart attitude. The older brother likely could claim to be a success with

104

the first two but a miserable failure at the third. His heartless obedience caused his deep self-pity.

Passive Appreciation

But other things contributed to the older brother's pain. One of them was passive appreciation.

In his book *The Ten Top Mistakes Leaders Make*, Hans Finzel includes a chapter entitled "The Absence of Affirmation." He relates the story of Keith, who quit his job as a salesman to take a white-collar desk job. When asked how things were going on the new job, Keith replied, "I feel worthless. There is nothing that I do right the first time, because everything is new to me." Then he added, "I lap up every little word of encouragement like a thirsty puppy. It's the only thing that keeps me going."[1]

As the old song says, "Little things mean a lot." Haven't you suspected your friends and family are guilty of passive appreciation? It's not that they don't appreciate you; they've just neglected to tell you how much. They love you but they just haven't been vocal in expressing it. Your boss appreciates the good job you do at work but he just forgets to pat you on the back now and then. That's passive appreciation.

Apparently the older prodigal endured a lack of expressed appreciation for years. But when the younger prodigal came home, the faithful son had all he could take. He complained to his father, "Look! All these years I've been slaving for you and never disobeyed your orders. Yet you never gave me even a young goat so I could celebrate with my friends" (v. 29).

No Pat on the Back

The older brother couldn't believe it. For years he had kept his father's commandments. He had worked long and hard in the fields. He had been the model of religious decorum. And yet neither his father nor anyone else ever patted him on the back.

The crabgrass kid was never center stage, never in the limelight. He was never thanked for his service. Nobody ever gave him a party. He was never allowed (as he saw it) to celebrate with his friends, and you can be sure they were as self-righteous as he was. I put in the phrase "as he saw it" because we're never told that the father wouldn't allow him to celebrate with his friends.

Does the work you do at home or church go largely unnoticed? Is there no one who appreciates you? The pastor never recognizes you from the pulpit. Your husband never thanks you for keeping your house in tiptop condition. People around us can be insensitive at times. But don't let that be justification for a pity party.

Do you grumble and complain when someone else gets the better parking place? Do you fester inside because someone else gets the recognition you deserve? If you do, you aren't surviving a prodigal; you're becoming one.

Repressed Association

As he continued to pour out his venom on the father, the older prodigal said, "But when this son of yours who has squandered your property with prostitutes comes home, you kill the fattened calf for him!" (v. 30).

What sarcasm! He couldn't even bring himself to call the prodigal his brother. He referred to him as "this son of yours." He repressed his association with his own flesh and blood. Why? Because of resentment for the gracious treatment the prodigal received from the father.

The psychology of self-pity produces a hurt so bad that you can't bring yourself to admit your family relationship. When your hurt is so deep you can only express it by denial. When you've been hurting so long that, when the valve finally blows, you deny you even have a relationship with those who have hurt you.

You men understand this. Your son plays Little League baseball. When he hits the home run that wins the game, you come home to tell Mom. With your hands clenched to your lapels, proudly you announce, "My son. My son hit the home run that won the game. My son."

The next game your little slugger hits another home run, but this time the ball crashes through Mrs. Brown's window. You come home to tell Mom. Distancing yourself you question, "Do you know what your kid did?"

Repressed association. It's human nature. But in the case of the older brother, it arose from self-pity. He was so destitute of love, so bereft of compassion that he was forced to say "your son" instead of "my brother."

The Stuff of a Pity-Full Life

Are you having difficulty claiming Christian kinship to someone of a different ethnic background? Maybe you're troubled by the thought of being spiritually related to someone in another denominational group. Whatever the case, sometimes we are so filled with self-pity that we repress our association with other believers.

We have little compassion for this pastor or that TV preacher. We have nothing but criticism for the Bible teacher who understands Scripture differently than we do. We deny any kinship in Christ with others because they receive the attention we'd like to receive.

Let me be blatantly honest. All of us have had our little self-pity parties. But most get over them quickly. Some people, however, have engaged in self-pity so long it's become the stuff of life for them. They see everything that happens in the church as a personal slap in the face. They just know nobody in the family appreciates them. The next time the pastor mentions someone's name from the pulpit, they know it won't be theirs.

Have you been getting slapped around in your church family lately? Has the credit for work you did gone to another? Have accolades been passed around, but passed over you? Deep down inside, are you feeling the pain of self-pity?

Someone Cares

If so, there's hope for the hurting heart. Someone cares for you. "Cast all your anxiety on him [Jesus] because he cares for you" (1 Pet. 5:7).

Someone notices your hurting heart. "Do not let your hearts be troubled. Trust in God; trust also in me" (John 14:1).

Someone really can provide peace to your troubled heart. "Peace I leave with you; my peace I give you. I do not give to you as the world gives. Do not let your hearts be troubled and do not be afraid" (John 14:27).

The Lord Jesus has a marvelously sympathetic heart. He knows the hurting heart of the prodigal, and He knows the hurting heart of the older brother. Robert Frost once said, "There never was any heart truly great and generous, that was not also tender and compassionate." Of no one is that more certain than Jesus.

If you have a hurting heart today, don't wallow in self-pity as the older brother did. Instead, give your hurts to the Lord Jesus. Ask Him to bear your heaviest burden. Ask Him to help you through your jealousy over another person. Ask Him to pull you tightly to His chest so you can feel the strength and warmth of His love. Pray that He will remove all traces of self-pity from your life, because being a prodigal of self-pity is as destructive as being a prodigal of self-interest.

You can only survive the prodigals in your life if you don't join them. Give up your self-pity and enjoy the celebration.

Notes

1. Hans Finzel, *The Top Ten Mistakes Leaders Make.* (Wheaton, IL: Victor Books, 1994), 56,57.

Chapter 11

SHRIVELED SOULS

"Join the party"

While it's easy for us to get caught up in Jesus' story, to see applications to it all around us—in our family, our church, our community—it's important to remember who His original audience was. The Pharisees and scribes, the super-religious leaders of Jesus' day, grumbled when they saw Jesus eating with sinners. Jesus told this story in response to their concerns. Read again verses one through three of Luke 15 that sets up the three parables Jesus told in verses four through 32.

These self-righteous leaders must have felt pretty good about the first part of Jesus' parable. After all, they could see prodigals all around them. No doubt they understood the prodigal son to be the tax collectors and sinners. Perhaps Jesus was coming to His senses.

But the Pharisees and scribes could never have guessed the turn Jesus' story took with the older brother. Jesus' parable must have blindsided them when He so graphically depicted them as older brothers. They just didn't see it coming.

Israel's religious leaders had shown no concern for lawbreakers in their midst. They were not compassionate people. They treated the tax collectors and sinners as outcasts, people to be snarled at as they passed by. They were older brothers, all of them.

Jealous Aggravation

As the Master Storyteller came to the end of His vignette about the elder prodigal, He showed us what happens when we are so taken up with correctly crossing every theological "t" and dotting every moral "i" that we fail to see God working in the lives of others. The crabgrass kid was so absorbed in himself and his work that he was surprised when the younger prodigal came home. He was self-indignant and angry when he heard the music and dancing. He succumbed to self-pity when he said, "You never gave me even a young goat so I could celebrate with my friends."

But the worst evidence of Pharisaism came when the older brother said, "But when this son of yours who has squandered your property with prostitutes comes home, you kill the fattened calf for him!" (Luke 15:30). This was nothing short of an outburst of jealous aggravation.

The older prodigal was so jealous of his younger brother that he accused him of things which, while probably true, he had no way of knowing.

Think for a moment. The prodigal had just returned. The older brother had not yet seen him. When the party began the older brother approached the house but refused to enter. Quickly the older son let loose his tirade against the father and his brother. He accused his younger brother of wasting the family inheritance with prostitutes. But how did he know? How could he know? He hadn't been told. He hadn't talked with his brother. How was it possible for him to know this?

Maybe he knew because beneath his self-righteous exterior he knew his own heart. Of course his younger brother spent everything on harlots. The older brother knew he would have done the same. He was guilty of transferring his inner desires onto his younger brother.

He judged the prodigal without knowing the facts. His resentment of his father and brother drove him to jealous aggravation. He blurted out what was in his heart—a hurting heart. He spoke what was on his mind—a bruised psyche. The Pharisees and the older brother were just as the Lord Jesus described them—whitewashed sepulchers, looking good on the outside but rotten on the inside (Matt. 23:27).

Shriveled Souls

Self-righteousness is the sin of a shriveled soul. The very word says it all—we are self right, right with ourselves. But we are not God's standard of righteousness; Jesus Christ is. Measuring ourselves by our own standard is like using a crooked ruler to draw a straight line. It can't be done.

The scribes and Pharisees were very good at this. Scribes were a class of learned men who made a systematic study of the Torah, the Law of Moses. They became Torah experts and saw themselves as the preservers and educators of the Law. They were very self-right-eous, like the older brother.

The name "Pharisee" is equivalent to the Hebrew word *hasidim*, meaning "the separated ones." Today Hasidic Jews—the ones wear-ing black hats and coats and long curls at their sideburns—are the spiritual descendants of the Pharisees.

Josephus, a Jewish historian and contemporary of Jesus, described the Pharisees as a body of Jews who professed to be more religious than the rest. We could hardly suggest a better definition today. Like the older brother, they saw themselves as righteous above all others.

But like the older brother, the Pharisees and scribes had shriveled souls. Their interpretations and amplifications of the Law were all calculated to display their righteousness. Some of those amplifica-tions had little bearing on reality.

Cockeyed Righteousness

They remind me of a book by Dick Hyman entitled *Cockeyed Americana*. In this book, Hyman catalogs some of the laws and statutes that were on the books in cities and states around America. Likely some of these laws have been repealed by now (I hope), but the author included such cockeyed statutes as:

—in Arizona it's unlawful to hunt or shoot a camel;

—in Virginia it's against the law to have a bathtub in the house (it must be in the yard);

—in Detroit, Michigan, you're not permitted to hitch a crocodile to a fire hydrant;

—in Trout Creek, Utah, pharmacists are not permitted to sell gunpowder as a headache cure; and

—in Lincoln, Nebraska, it's against the law for burglars to use the front door (presumably the back door is acceptable).[1]

Every time I read *Cockeyed Americana*, these self-righteous Pharisees and scribes come to mind. Their restrictions didn't make much sense either, but they did provide the reason for Jesus including the older brother in His parable.

What do you believe makes you righteous? That's an important question because your answer will determine whether or not you enjoy fellowship with the father as the younger prodigal did or you endure estrangement from the father as the older prodigal did. He based righteousness on what he did, how faithful he was, how straight as an arrow he lived. But his self-righteousness was that of a shriveled soul. Compared to the Father's forgiveness, all our righteousness is as filthy rags.

If we truly want to be righteous, we must submit ourselves to the standard of Jesus Christ, a standard by which the Bible says we miserably fall short (Rom. 3:23). However, recognizing we fall short is the first step in measuring up. We can then accept Christ's death on our behalf to appease God's wrath against us for sin, accept His forgiveness, and let God change our lives forever.

The older brother never saw this. When the righteousness of Christ becomes our righteousness, not only will we meet God's standard but we'll exceed our own as well.

Two Sons; Two Prodigals

Jesus' third parable featured three characters for a good reason. In Jesus' mind, the father had two prodigals, not one. One wandered away from his father, but returned. One never left, but was far from his father nonetheless. Don't let this fact escape you. At the story's end, one son was in the house enjoying the party. The other son was outside being miserable.

None of us likes to think of ourselves as prodigals. We don't like to think of ourselves as older brothers either. But it betrays deep psychological hurt when we become so filled with self-pity and self-righteousness that we won't enjoy the family celebration.

Perhaps the Savior included the older brother in this parable because He knew the hurt many of us endure. He knew many of His followers would allow bitterness and resentment to build inside them. He also knew what had to be done.

If you're like the older brother, if resentment toward a family member, a church member, or a neighbor has been boiling inside of you, flush it out. Get rid of it before it bruises your mind. Say good-bye to resentment before it oppresses your soul. It will eat you alive and destroy your life, just as it did the older brother.

Exchange Bitterness for Joy

Paul tells us, "Get rid of all bitterness, rage and anger, brawling and slander, along with every form of malice. Be kind and compassionate to one another, forgiving each other, just as in Christ God forgave you" (Eph. 4:31-32). It's like one of those gun buy-back programs that have become popular in American cities. You take a weapon that can kill you, turn it in at the police station, and they give you some cash for it that you can buy food or clothes with. You simply exchange what is harmful for what is helpful. The Spirit of God will help you do that, if you ask Him. What are you waiting for?

We don't know whether the older brother was salvaged or not. The story doesn't tell us. We don't know how he responded to the father's call to leave his bitterness behind and join in the life of the family. We don't know if the older brother survived the prodigal in his life.

But the door was left wide open for him as it is for you. Bitterness is sin. Resentment is sin. Self-righteousness is sin. You only deal with them adequately when you confess them to God and make them right with the one against whom you have sinned.

Is there some brother or sister you need to visit? Is there someone you should call or write today? Don't delay. Get it right with God, and then get it right with that friend or family member. Get rid of your hurt. It's the only way to enjoy the Father's family.

Wouldn't it be a shame for one prodigal to come home again to enjoy the life of the family and for another prodigal to be there all the time and be left out? Don't let bitterness or self-righteousness keep you outside when the celebration is going on inside. Get rid of them and come on in and join the party.

Notes

1. Dick Hyman, *Cockeyed Americana*. (Brattleboro, VT: The Stephen Greene Press, 1972).

AN EMPTY LIFE
Kelly Francis

Kelly Francis was a prodigal daughter. It was hard to talk about it for years, but considering what God has done for her now, she's happy to share her story with you. It's a real story of a real prodigal.

"I was raised in a Southern Baptist church," Kelly remembers. "And when I say raised, I mean 'raised.'" Kelly's parents saw that her brothers and sisters and she were in church every time the doors were opened. That meant they attended every Sunday morning, every Sunday evening and every midweek service on Wednesday night. They also were faithful in helping out at the first-Tuesday visitation every month. Kelly and her kin were real church folks.

But there's a huge difference between being raised in church and being happy there. As Kelly admits, "I rebelled when I was 16. I walked away from everything I knew to be true." Kelly decided church was no fun, and she wanted to have fun in the other world, the world without God. She vowed she would never return to church.

Kelly remembers that her parents and other church people "looked down their noses at me." It was because of the lifestyle she chose for herself. "For ten years I lived a life independent of God (so I thought). Drinking, smoking, drugs and promiscuity filled my life. I was really proud of my independent lifestyle. I didn't need anyone."

Dangerous Self-Sufficiency

Self-sufficient Kelly bought into the misguided rhetoric of the feminist movement. She was a modern woman. She lived alone. She partied every night. And she held down a prestigious job. She had it all, or so she thought. No one would tell her what to do, what to think, what to believe.

What Kelly didn't realize is that's exactly what others were doing. She remembers, "Like the prodigal in Jesus' story, I wanted to make it on my own. I listened to every TV ad, every woman's magazine article that convinced me I didn't need God; I was enough all by myself. But there's one thing the television and those magazine articles didn't tell me—how empty my life would become."

Today Kelly is grateful for what God did in her life while she was on the run from Him. She says, "The Lord never let go of me, as evidenced by the fact that I'm still alive! I watched friends go to prison, suffer terminal health problems due to their lifestyle, and others fall into depression and despair." The magazines and television also failed to mention that!

Trying Religion

Kelly knew her life had to change. She thought what she needed was religion in her life. She remembers, "I tried getting back into the church, visiting over 50 churches in two years (everything from New Age to Catholic!). I thought that would make my life better." But nothing seemed to help.

How tragic that Kelly didn't read the story of the prodigal son and take note that the prodigal wasn't just going home; he was going home to the father. Kelly didn't just need to go back to church; she needed to come home to her Heavenly Father.

Frustrated by the lack of answers to be found in formal religion, Kelly's life continued to be estranged from her family, from God, and from the law. She remembers, "It wasn't until I was convinced my life was meaningless that I remembered what a Sunday School teacher told me many years before. She said, 'No matter where you go, or what you do, God always knows and always loves you anyway.'" Kelly wasn't sure that God could look past everything she had done in ten years since she turned her back on Him, but she figured it was worth a try. She thought, "If He couldn't really love me, then what's the harm in having tried?"

180-Degree Turnaround

Kelly prayed what she could remember of the sinner's prayer and told God that she'd like to change but was sure she couldn't succeed on her own. That's what God was waiting to hear. That's what He's waiting to hear from every prodigal.

Kelly's life has done a 180-degree turnaround. Not uncommon for prodigals. Six months after she gave in and returned to the Lord, she met the man who would become her husband. Kelly rededicated her life to serving the Lord. She is now raising a Christian family, is active in her home church, and is involved in full-time ministry for the Lord.

When God gets the attention of a prodigal, He really gets their attention. Their lives are never the same again.

Part Three

THE LOVING FATHER

When You Are Squeezed Between Runaway and Stay-at-Home Prodigals

Chapter 12

RECOGNIZE YOUR PRODIGAL'S REAL TARGET

"It's not you, it's God!"

We have focused on the younger son and his desire to leave his Jewish home. We have seen his stupidity and his sensibility. He came back to the father and his family. We have also given some thought to the older son and his refusal to accept his sibling back.

It's time now to go back to the parable and see the role the father plays in all of this. If like the father in Jesus' story, you are squeezed between two prodigals or have one or the other in your family, how will you respond? What lessons can be learned about handling strained relationships with your children, your friends, your church family? Let's focus on what we can learn from the father.

Are you at home waiting for your prodigal to return? Are you having a tough time coping with your own feelings? Likely you are. Parents or spouses of prodigals frequently are riddled with guilt. You feel awful about your runaway, and down deep inside you blame yourself. If so, then here is an insight that is especially for you. This may keep you from driving yourself crazy. Here's what the story of the prodigal teaches us about parents. It's not you that your prodigal is mad at; it's God.

Prodigalism Is a Personal Choice

The truth is, we do contribute to the feelings of our prodigal. In fact, we may be partly to blame for the lifestyle they chose. But Jesus' story teaches us that, ultimately, prodigalism is a personal choice—their choice.

In recent years our courtrooms have showcased the "I'm not responsible" syndrome. The Menendez brothers kill their parents, but it's not their fault because they were abused as children. A young man shoots a convenience store clerk in cold blood, but the killer is not responsible. He grew up in a violent neighborhood. What else would you expect but violent behavior?

Some time back ABC aired a special by *20/20*'s John Stossel called "The Blame Game." It was a fascinating look at the "It's not my fault" thinking that permeates American society. Nobody is responsible; everybody is a victim. This likely was brought to our national consciousness when an older woman sued McDonald's because she was burned by spilling a hot cup of coffee in her lap. The jury awarded her $2.9 million, which later a judge reduced to a paltry $640,000. She finally settled for an undisclosed amount.

The report also featured the story of a grown man who was riding his bicycle at night without a light. It was dark, of course, and the man was accidentally struck by a Jeep. He was fine but his lawyer assisted him to sue, not the driver of the Jeep, but the company who made the bicycle for not warning him that riding your bike at night without a light might be dangerous. Sounds ludicrous, I know, but wait until you hear the result. The jury awarded him $7 million. The bicycle company had to cough it up because they didn't put a warning label on the bike such as: "Warning. If you ride at night, you need a light."

These things make sane people sick. And yet such examples are in the newspaper almost every day. At some point, we adults are going to have to take responsibility for our actions. But the same is true for our teens. When a teen decides he or she doesn't want to live at home anymore and leaves the parents without a trace, that teen is responsible for his or her own actions. When a man leaves his wife and kids to take up with some gal at the office, that husband is responsible for his own actions. We have to begin acting like adults; we have to begin to take responsibility for our actions.

Regardless of how you as a parent or spouse may have contributed to the troubles of your prodigal, there is an underlying truth that surfaces in the parable of the prodigal son. The lad was responsible for what happened to him after he left home. He was on his own and he was responsible.

But there is another equally important truth wedded to the first in this story—a truth for all those waiting the return of prodigals. Here it is: You are not the object of your spouse's prodigalism. You are not the object of your son or daughter's anger. You may feel it keenly, but if you're to survive the prodigals in your life, you must recognize that their prodigalism is directed toward someone else, not primarily toward you. Prodigalism, like all other sin, is ultimately always directed against God.

Sinning Against Heaven

In Jesus' parable did you notice whom the prodigal confessed he had sinned against? In verse 21 he said, "Father, I have sinned against heaven and against you." Heaven first, father second.

For the longest time that expression troubled me. I read this story again and again. I knew what it meant that the prodigal had sinned against his father. He had disrespected him, dishonored him. But what did he mean that he had sinned against heaven?

It's evident the expression "against heaven" meant against God in heaven. The Jews found it difficult to speak God's name. They used expressions like "against heaven" when they referred to sinning against God. But how did the prodigal sin against God? What could this mean?

Similar expressions occur several places in the Bible. Perhaps they will help us understand what the prodigal meant.

The Prince of Egypt

Joseph was the favorite son of Jacob. God revealed in dreams that Joseph would be divinely used in a very special way. But like the older brother in Jesus' parable, Joseph's brothers resented him. In fact, they hated him. Jacob gave too much attention to Joseph and too little to them.

Thus, the brothers sold Joseph into slavery as a young man. An Egyptian named Potiphar purchased him to be his young Hebrew slave. Eventually Joseph would become the prince of Egypt, next to the great Pharaoh himself. But while he was still a servant in Potiphar's house, Potiphar's wife got a good look at the handsome Joseph. She liked what she saw and attempted to seduce him.

Joseph refused again and again. But when she grabbed him by his coat and begged him to sleep with her, do you remember what Joseph said? When her advances were rebuffed, he said, "How then could I do such a wicked thing and sin against God?" (Gen. 39:9).

His primary concern was not sinning against Potiphar. He wasn't concerned about sinning against the woman, or even himself. Joseph's concern was sinning against God. Did Joseph recognize something many of us have forgotten?

King David

David's sin with Bathsheba was a disgraceful thing. The king could have any legitimate thing he wanted, but what he wanted was illegitimate. He wanted another man's wife. He lusted after Bathsheba, slept with her and sent her away (2 Sam. 11:4). When he discovered that his sin had produced a child, he called for Bathsheba's husband, Uriah the Hittite, to return from fighting the Ammonites. He wanted it to appear as if this was Uriah's child.

But his plan backfired and David sent Uriah back to the fighting, this time to the battlefront to insure that he would die. David committed the double sins of adultery and conspiracy to murder.

But when he poured out his heart and confessed his sin, recorded in Psalm 51, do you remember what he said? His exact words to God were: "For I know my transgressions, and my sin is always before me. Against you, you only, have I sinned and done what is evil in your sight" (Ps. 51:3-4).

What about Bathsheba? More to the point, what about Uriah? He was dead because of David's sin! How could David say to God, "Against you, you only, have I sinned"? Did David remember something many of us have forgotten?

Saul of Tarsus

Saul of Tarsus was a strict Pharisee and a contemporary of Christ. After our Lord's ascension into heaven, the Gospel began to spread like wildfire. This enraged Saul because he viewed Christianity as a perversion of Judaism.

Saul was on his way to Damascus, Syria, to put people in chains who had trusted Jesus as their Messiah. He wanted to drag them back to Jerusalem and punish them for their faith. But en route a bright light beamed down from heaven and a voice said, "Saul, Saul, why do you persecute my people?"

Is that what the voice said? Don't be so sure; it's not at all what God said. The voice said, "Saul, Saul, why do you persecute me?" (Acts 9:4). Does the Lord Jesus remember something many of us have forgotten?

If you're battling feelings of guilt because you have a prodigal in your family, remember this: Sin is, ultimately, always directed against God. That's what Joseph remembered, and David remembered, and Jesus remembered—that maybe we've forgotten.

When your prodigal sins against you, it's not really you they are directing their vengeance toward. They are sinning against God. That's what makes it sin—it's ultimately always directed against God.

When we sin, do we involve other people? Frequently we do, but we always involve God. When we sin, do we hurt other people? Yes we do, but we ultimately hurt our Heavenly Father. In the final analysis, sin is always directed against God.

The prodigal son realized that. In fact, that may be the greatest lesson he learned while away from home. That's why his confession began, "I have sinned against heaven." He knew he had sinned against God.

Involving Others in Our Sin

If a man cheats in paying his income taxes, he sins against God. If a wife is unfaithful to her husband, she sins against God. If people engage in premarital or extramarital sex, they sin against God. The rape of a woman is a sin against God. The abuse of a child is a sin against God. The misuse of power is a sin against God.

I don't mean to diminish the hurt experienced by an abused child. If you've been abused as a young child, you know how real the hurt is. If you've been the victim of a rapist, your pain is genuine and unimaginable. No sensitive person would suggest that it doesn't hurt when you learn your spouse has been unfaithful to you. It hurts deeply.

But part of Satan's strategy has always been to desensitize us to sin. He wants us to think that we sin only against people, and they'll get over it. But ultimately sin is always directed against God, and even consenting adults have to come to grips with what that means.

Have you wrestled with what the prodigal learned in the pig-pen—that sin is always directed against God? The prodigal knew his treatment of the father was wrong, but he also knew he was not venting his anger against the father alone. He did not flaunt his arrogance merely in the face of the father. He had also been angry and arrogant against God, and he came to realize that this was his greater sin.

The same is true with us. We may sin against our parents, our children or our spouse. We may sin against our pastor, our church or ourselves. But our sin is, ultimately, always directed against God. Your children who have sinned against you have not been so angry at you as they have been angry at God.

Insensitivity to Sin

Vance Havner said, "We do not have healthy hatred of sin today because we have no proper sense of the holiness of God." Said another way, we have a diminished appreciation for the holiness of God, and thus we have a diminished appreciation for the heinousness of sin.

Sin is no joke. It's an offense against a holy God. It devastates our lives and robs our righteousness. Viewing our sin from God's vantage point is the first step in restoring a godly shudder at sin. That's a much-needed shudder today.

Do you see why one of your major needs is to pray for your prodigals? Pray for their health and safety; they need that. But they have a much greater need. If they have sinned against you, they have ultimately sinned against God. Your prayers should key on the power of the Holy Spirit to bring them to their senses, to convict them of their sin, to open their eyes to the fact that their anger and arrogance have not been directed toward you alone. Pray that they understand their sin is always against God.

The Prodigal's Deeper Agenda

Do you want to survive the prodigals in your life? Get a headlock on the prodigal's insight in Jesus' family portrait. If you're feeling twinges of guilt because your prodigal has left you, get ahold of Jesus' perspective. Your prodigal hasn't sinned just against you; even worse, they've sinned against God. They didn't leave home to punish you; they had a much deeper agenda than that.

Okay, you want to be a survivor. How will you do it? You're feeling twinges of guilt because your spouse left you. You're beginning to understand that you may have said or done things that contributed to your daughter leaving home. What should you do?

Don't spend your nights swimming in guilt; spend them in prayer instead. Your lonely nights will be much more profitable if you commit your spouse or your child to God. Recognize that sin, even the sin of a prodigal, is ultimately against God.

It's not about you; it's about God. Your prodigals didn't want to hurt you as much as they wanted to hurt the Heavenly Father. They must return to God before they can return to you. That's what you should pray for

That's how to survive the prodigals in your life. Ask God to care for them, to confront them, but more than anything else to convict them of sin. They sinned against heaven before they sinned against you. Pray that they will return to God, for when a prodigal returns to the Father, they'll return to you as well.

Chapter 13

WELCOME YOUR PRODIGAL HOME

"Let your love show"

You've prayed, you've waited, you now recognize the true object of your prodigal's anger, and you're ready to receive your prodigal home again. But when your eyes meet theirs for the first time, what will you do? What will you say? If you're to survive the prodigals in your life, you have to learn how to let your love show.

More than a hundred years ago George Matheson wrote the words to a beautiful hymn: "O Love that wilt not let me go, I rest my weary soul in Thee; I give Thee back the life I owe, that in Thine ocean depths its flow may richer, fuller be."

It's almost as if the prodigal were whispering in the hymn writer's ear. He easily could have said these words to his father.

Matheson, of course, was writing about the love of God. But the prodigal's compassionate father is very much like God. He's the perfect example of how to receive a prodigal home again. Like God the Father, he let his love show.

For years psychology students have been introduced to studies on compassion. Some of these have been done in orphanages where infants were dying despite adequate nutrition and care. The studies concluded these children died from a lack of being cuddled. They died because they lacked demonstrable love. Their attendants fed and changed them because it was their duty. The rest of the time the infants were left alone.

These students quickly learned the importance of love. They concluded that infants are born with a deep need, a need that a full stomach alone cannot meet. Sounds like the prodigal son, doesn't it?

The runaway prodigal could not be a whole person without his father's compassion. Even though he came to his senses and returned home, the prodigal would have been incomplete without the compassion of the father.

Seeing the Father in the Verbs

For more than two decades I taught young preachers how to craft sermons. I always counseled them to pay close attention to the verbs in a passage. That's where the action is, and wherever the action is, the sermon is.

Luke 15:20 is filled with action. In fact, there are five action verbs in this verse that reveal a great deal about the father. They also teach us how to receive a prodigal home again.

Here are the words of Jesus: "But while he was still a long way off, his father saw him and was filled with compassion for him; he ran to his son, threw his arms around him and kissed him" (v. 20).

Do you see your biological or earthly father in this verse? Maybe not. Not everyone is privileged to have a loving father in this life. Your father may have physically, sexually or verbally abused you. He may have been mean and uncaring. He may have come home drunk every night or not come home at all.

Many fathers today aren't what God intended them to be. But even if you don't see your earthly father in Luke 15:20, see your Heavenly Father. He's the Father who loves sinners. He's the God who awaits the return of every prodigal.

Let's investigate more closely how the father let his love show when the prodigal came home again.

The Father Saw His Son

"But while he was still a long way off, his father saw him."

How did the father have the good fortune of spotting his prodigal at just the right moment? Did he look out the window, casually glance across the fields, and gasp at his good luck? I don't think so.

The father saw his son because he was watching for him. From the moment the prodigal stormed out of the house, day and night the father prayed for his son's return. Loving fathers do that. They pray daily for their prodigals and constantly look for their return. It's how they let their love show.

One of my fondest childhood memories was visiting my Grandma and Grandpa Corbin's house. We always drove down a narrow driveway alongside the house when we visited. That meant Grandma said good-bye standing at the back door. She would wave again and again until we drove out of the driveway. But when we got to the front of the house, almost magically she appeared at the front door. It didn't matter how quickly we got to the end of the drive, my grandmother always beat us. She was there watching and waving as we drove off.

Grandma had to run from that back door to the front, but never once did she fail to be there, waving good-bye as we drove away. It's how grandmothers let their love show.

I think of her every time I read about this father. He was in the habit of looking for his prodigal, scouting the horizon every day for him. The son would never beat him to the door; the father was always there, watching for his return.

Don't ever stop looking for your prodigal. Expect him or her to come home every day; look for them every night. If you want to survive, believe God will bring them to their senses.

Never give up hope. Distance cannot dim the eyes of love.

The Father Loved His Son

Jesus said, "His father saw him and was filled with compassion for him."

It doesn't stretch believability that the father loved his son, at least it wouldn't if the son hadn't treated him so poorly. But the character of the father would not permit the conduct of the son to diminish his love.

Compassion is having your pain in my heart. The father knew what this meant. He did not love his son out of parental duty; he genuinely cared for his prodigal. He did not love him because the son returned home. He loved him the whole time the boy was gone. He never stopped loving him. He did not love him because he sensed his son's confession was genuine. He loved him before the son had opportunity to confess his sin. That's the way love is; that's the way it should show.

Don't love your prodigal only after you've said those four little words that give us so much pleasure—"I told you so." Love them as this father loved his son. Love your prodigal unconditionally as God loves you. When your prodigal comes home again, let your love show.

The Father Reclaimed His Son

How old do you suppose this father was? In Bible times families were begun much later in life than they are today. Remember Abraham and Sarah? The father in this story was likely no spring chicken anymore. Yet Jesus said he ran to meet his son. Oriental sheiks and wealthy landowners don't run. It's not becoming to their dignified position. Still, this father ran.

The Master Storyteller said, "His father saw him and was filled with compassion for him; he ran to his son." Picture arthritic knees bending as the father ran. Imagine feeble lungs expanding and contracting as he ran. Hear the rickety joints cracking. His eyes welled up with tears when he spotted his wayward prodigal. Age and dignity yielded as the father's heart yearned to embrace his son. He didn't make his son's return as difficult as possible; he made it as easy as possible. He went out of the house and retrieved him. He left behind the comfort and security of his home to reclaim his sinful son. That's how to let your love show.

But isn't that what our Heavenly Father did for us? Jesus Christ left the glory and privileges of heaven behind, came to our sinful environment and retrieved us because of the Father's great love for us. He came and got us; He rescued us. He left His home for us, so that we could come home again with Him.

The Father Embraced His Son

Jesus continued to paint His family portrait. This is one of the most tender scenes in the Bible. "But while he was still a long way off, his father saw him and was filled with compassion for him; he ran to his son, threw his arms around him and kissed him."

Most North Americans are not "touching" people. We don't do a lot of casual embracing. We shake hands, do a high five or just say something clever like "Hey" or "Whassup?" But in the Middle East embracing is the traditional way of greeting one another. An embrace and a kiss on each cheek is the customary welcome. I have friends in Israel who greet me this way each time I visit them. It's a much more personal way to say hello than the Western way.

But the embrace this father gave his runaway son was not the embrace of custom. It was the embrace of affection. It wasn't just a greeting. It was his way of letting the love show. The father gave his son the mother of all bear hugs. The father was beside himself with joy. He had to express it. He wanted the younger prodigal to know that it was okay for him to come home.

The Father Kissed His Son

The final display of the father's love was his kiss. After constant searching, the father left the house, ran to his returning son, embraced him heartily and kissed him again and again.

While it may have been one long progressive embrace, the grammar indicates the father planted a series of kisses on his son. The prefix of the verb tells us there was much kissing. The father kissed the prodigal again and again. He kissed him tenderly, fervently and repeatedly. These were kisses of genuine affection. The father wasn't afraid to let his love show.

When your prodigal returns home, whether that prodigal is a son, a spouse or whomever, prepare your heart for his or her return. Then receive your prodigal back for what he or she is—a lost treasure.

Let your love show. Don't wait for them to crawl back, tail between their legs. Go out and greet them. Lavish them with your love. Enjoy their return as the angels rejoice every time a sinner comes home to the Father (Luke 15:10).

You can survive the prodigals in your life. Take a page from this father's notebook. When your prodigal returns home, when your son or daughter calls from a distant city, when your prodigal spouse asks your forgiveness—let your love show. It's the cornerstone of survival.

Chapter 14

DISCOVER THE JOY
OF FORGIVENESS

"Enjoy forgiveness"

The prodigal left home to gain his freedom, to strike it rich, to be with people who really appreciated him. But everything he left home to find, the prodigal finally discovered when he came back home again. It was there all the time. He was just too blind to see it.

Teens walk away from their families for reasons that make sense to them, but they give little or no thought to the pain and hurt they cause their parents. Husbands walk away from their wives because Satan teases them elsewhere and tells them they deserve more. Wives do the same to husbands. The Devil has a way of creating an itch and then rubbing it into a burning irritation.

But Jesus' story is as much about the ointment that soothes as it is about the itch. When the prodigal returned home, the father applied the ointment of genuine forgiveness. It was something he didn't do sparingly or grudgingly. He was lavish. He forgave his son with genuine joy. Why? Because the father was a survivor and he had learned well that to fail to forgive is to fail to survive. If you want to survive the prodigals in your life, you have to learn to enjoy forgiveness.

Genuine joy always bursts into expression. Jesus' parable reveals some very unique ways the father expressed his joy. We may show our forgiveness in other ways, but the underlying elements are always there if we are to survive the prodigals in our life.

Joy in the heart makes happy hands and feet. Notice how the joy of forgiveness bubbled out of this father.

Slaves Scurrying

The excited father barked a series of quick orders to his household servants (Luke 15:22). This was the day he had longed for and prayed for. Now his son was home again and there were things to be done—done right away.

Back there in the pigpen surely the prodigal didn't expect his father to treat him in such a regal manner if he returned. That's because the selfish son only understood justice; he knew nothing of grace.

When a prodigal wanders from us, it's only the joy of forgiveness that enables us to treat them with kindness, even with regality. That's what God did. When He forgave us for walking out the door and living in sin, we were not treated as despised slaves; we were treated as forgiven sons. That's how to enjoy forgiving.

When your prodigal returns, do yourself a favor. Experience the joy of forgiveness. Make a fuss. Send some servants scurrying. Treat your wounded prodigal regally. You'll only have one opportunity to do so. You'll only regret it if you don't.

The Best Robe

Another evidence of the father's forgiving joy was the way he clothed his wayward son. He sent the servants to fetch the best robe. Quickly the tattered rags the boy wore in shame were covered with the most luxurious garment imaginable. The father wasted no time in helping the boy forget his foolish past.

In the original language this garment is called a stole. It was a stately garment, the finely woven outer garment that came down to the feet. It was certainly not everyday clothing; it wasn't even Sunday clothing. So special was this long robe that it was worn only by special people on special occasions.

The word *stole* is used nine times in the Bible. In Mark 12:38 and Luke 20:46 it refers to the long robes worn by the scribes. "Beware of the teachers of the law. They like to walk around in flowing robes." In Revelation 6:11 a white stole was given to each of the martyrs who were slain for the Word of God.

In Revelation 7:9,13 and twice in verse 14 the word relates to those who came out of the Great Tribulation and "washed their robes and made them white in the blood of the Lamb."

And in Mark 16:5 the stole was the robe of an angel. "As they entered the tomb, they saw a young man dressed in a white robe sitting on the right side...."

In the Bible this word is always used of a regal garment, worn by a splendid person (or by persons who thought they were splendid) on a regal occasion. There's no reason to believe it was any different in Jesus' parable.

The best robe was regal evidence of the joy of forgiveness. When the father forgave the prodigal, he did it with joy, he did it with style, he did it with the best he had. How we treat a returning prodigal says a lot to him or her about how much we've truly forgiven. Get your stole ready; there may be a prodigal at your door soon.

The Ring

The father's forgiving joy was also demonstrated by the exquisite ring he put on his son's hand. Jesus gave no detailed description of it, but it must have been stunning. Any ring less than spectacular would be out of character in this scene.

I have a ring that people frequently comment about. It's an oval-shaped cameo, about one-half inch in diameter. Into the cameo shell is intricately carved the head of a Roman centurion. I paid almost nothing for it because I bought it at a cameo factory near Naples, Italy. But while inexpensive, it is a very regal-looking ring. I can only imagine what this ring would mean to me if it had been given by a forgiving father.

The regal quality of the father's forgiveness permits us to speculate that this ring may have been a signet ring. A signet was used as the seal or signature of a king or head of a family. Every signet ring was a one-of-a-kind in order to prevent forgeries.

After Pharaoh put Joseph in charge of the land of Egypt, "Pharaoh took his signet ring from his finger and put it on Joseph's finger. He dressed him in robes of fine linen and put a gold chain around his neck" (Gen. 41:41-42).

The father put a ring on the prodigal's finger to prove the extent of his forgiveness. It symbolized the joy that forgiveness brought to the one who forgave. It demonstrated that just as it is more blessed to give than to receive, it is more blessed to forgive than to reprieve. The father didn't give his son a lecture. He didn't give him a reprieve. He gave him joyful forgiveness.

If you want to survive the prodigals in your life, learn to not just let it go. Learn to forgive them. Don't just forget it; forgive it. There's joy in forgiveness that forgetfulness will never know.

The Shoes

Then the father commanded his servants to bind shoes on his son's feet. These would have been sandals of the type worn in the Ancient Near East.

Three questions come to mind about these shoes. Why did the prodigal not have his own shoes? Why were shoes so important to the father? And why was it important that the servants put the sandals on the prodigal's feet?

Jesus didn't say the son's shoes were old. They didn't merely need to be cleaned or the thongs tightened. This boy had no shoes at all. He was a barefoot prodigal. We're not told what happened to the prodigal's shoes. Perhaps he sold them when he was hard up for cash. Maybe they simply wore out and he couldn't afford to replace them. Stomping around the pigpen would have ruined his shoes. Likely they had to be discarded.

But why not just let the son go barefoot? All the servants were barefoot, why not the prodigal? The answer is cultural. Being barefoot was a sign of slavery. Freemen never went barefoot in the Roman Empire. The father ordered shoes bound on his son's feet so everyone would know he was being received as a son, not as a slave. It was especially important his son knew this. It gave the father forgiving joy.

But why did the father tell the servants to tie the sandals on his son's feet? Why not hand them to the boy and tell him to put them on himself? Because that was a servant's job.

Remember John the Baptist's comment when he saw Jesus? He said, "He is the one who comes after me, the thongs of whose sandals I am not worthy to untie" (John 1:27). Unloosing sandals was not the job of a superior; it was the job of a servant

The jubilant father sent his servants scurrying when the prodigal returned home. He sent them scurrying for three symbols of authority, three status symbols, three evidences of his forgiveness—the best robe, the exquisite ring, and the shoes of a freeman.

Do you see how much fun the father was having? Such are the expressions of joy when one forgives. Forgiving is giving, but it's never losing! You can survive the prodigals in your life if you learn to experience the joy of forgiveness.

The Fattened Calf

The compassionate father expressed his forgiving joy in one final spectacular way. Luke 15:23 continues, "Bring the fattened calf and kill it. Let's have a feast and celebrate."

Poorer people lived hand to mouth. They could honestly pray, "Give us this day our daily bread." But wealthy people—like this father/landowner—had plenty to eat. In fact, wealthier people always kept a fattened calf for a special occasion.

This was no ordinary calf. It did not graze the hills of Palestine looking for a meager meal. The word *fattened* is a verbal adjective that means "fed with wheat." This calf was grain-fed, probably feed-lot-fed. This was a special calf, for a special person. Tonight they would eat and be merry.

But take note that it was not just the father and his son who enjoyed this celebration. All the servants joined them. There was corporate joy, shared joy. The joy that comes with forgiveness is too precious to experience alone. It must be spread around.

Do your prodigal children know how much you'll enjoy forgiving them? Does your runaway spouse believe he or she will be received home again with joy? You may not be experiencing difficulties with a prodigal now, but if you should in the future, what are you doing now that would send signals to your spouse or your children that, should they wander away from the family, they would be welcomed home with the joy of forgiveness?

Full Pardon

In 1974 the United Press International reported the saga of Vasily Khuyl, a Russian deserter who left the German front in 1944 and spent 30 years hiding in a pigpen in the Ukraine. The article said, "[Khuyl's] thirty years of hiding were terribly monotonous and the entire time could be expressed with a few verbs—sit, lie, eat, and look through a crack."

In 1949 the former Soviet Union granted amnesty for Soviet deserters, but Vasily Khuyl didn't know he could be forgiven just by going home again. He wasted his life in a pigpen because he didn't return home to receive a full pardon.

Does your prodigal believe they'll be received with the joy of forgiveness if they come home? Do they sense that you believe the best way to survive a prodigal is to forgive them? When your prodigal returns will there be a lecture or a party?

Let's cut right through to the heart of the issue. If your prodigal showed up at your door today, would you:

a) slam the door in his or her face;

b) speak but not let him or her in;

c) let him or her return but only after meeting certain conditions;

d) welcome your prodigal home without conditions or a trial period.

Be honest. How would you respond? Most of us would opt for "c." We would admit the prodigal back into our home, but there would be some changes made. They would have to toe the line. They would have to prove they were sorry for hurting us. They would have to meet stringent preconditions.

And yet we find none of that in Jesus' parable. No preconditions. No "If you do this, I'll receive you back." All we see is a compassionate father with open arms. Some people find it easier to forgive after they've gotten even. But God's forgiveness forbids getting even. When we forgive as God forgave, we forgive without rejection, without remorse, without retribution.

When Hurt Lingers

Some time ago I received a letter from a listener to *Back to the Bible*. After hearing a message I gave on forgiving prodigals, she poured out her heart to me, sharing something of the joy and pain of surviving a prodigal. Here are some excerpts from her letter shared by permission:

I have two grown children—a son and a daughter. When my daughter was a teenager, she ran away from home. For nearly three years we did not know where she was.

As a parent, I know the feelings of the father in the parable of the prodigal son. There are sleepless nights, wondering, fearing what may be happening to your wayward child. There is constant yearning to hear her footsteps coming through the door. There is constant prayer on your lips for God to bring her home.

Our daughter did come home. As well as I can know my heart, I have forgiven her fully. But through the nearly 20 years that have followed, her father's hurt still lingers. And her brother continues to hold her rebellious teen years against her. Forgiveness and acceptance of the returning prodigal does not come easy.

Does this woman's letter reflect your experience? Forgiveness and acceptance of a returning prodigal do not come easy. But if you're to face life together, you must experience the joy of forgiveness together.

Lavish your forgiveness with joy and your prodigal will never question whether or not you have forgiven them. It's how to survive the prodigals in your life. Enjoy forgiving them. Show them you enjoy it.

THE PRODIGAL SPOUSE

John McNally

"As long as I can remember, the most important thing to me was to be loved and accepted. I discovered early that how I looked, how I performed in athletics, and how much charm I turned on made a huge difference in how much I accomplished my two primary goals. As a result, I have used these things to get what I wanted from people for nearly 50 years."

That admission was from John McNally, a prodigal husband. He was indeed a great athlete. His abilities on the football field turned the heads of many college scouts; he got a lot of press. And he was handsome. "Getting girls" was never a problem. Schoolwork and grades were never an issue either. Good jobs and prestigious positions were always open to him. He had the world by the tail on a downhill swing. He could get whatever he wanted, and he used anyone and anything to his advantage.

New Life; Old Habits

John laments, "I can't believe how greatly deceived my heart was. I was a religious person and had a moral sense of conscience. In fact, I had planned to go to college to become a minister even though I wasn't even a Christian at the time."

As a young teen John met Maggie Mitchell. Because he was athletic, handsome, and all that a 16-year-old girl could want, Maggie fell in love instantly. John became her life. As high school sweethearts they dated for three years and, after graduation, were married. Six years later, both at age 24, John and Maggie received Christ as their Savior. It was quite a transformation. John's heart burned with the desire to share his faith with the world. Together they began to grow in spiritual things and their sole desire was to glorify the Savior in every area of their lives. John and Maggie were building a wonderful life together, and then it happened.

Everything in life began to unravel.

John was working as a leasing agent when he met a woman who had recently been divorced. He shared his faith with her and she professed to trust Christ as Savior. But what she was really looking for was not a relationship with the Lord; she was looking for a relationship with John.

As is often the case when something wild and forbidden comes into our life, John's ego kicked into high gear. He liked the attention this woman gave him, because she was feeding all those things that were so important to John. That's when he got his eyes off the Savior and onto this woman. John began a secret affair with her that lasted nearly four years.

The High Price of Sin

As he now recalls, "The battle between my flesh and my spirit raged the entire time. There were many nights that I would come home from work after being with this woman and kneel beside the beds of my children, weeping and asking God to deliver me from my sin." John knew he was not pleasing the Lord, nor was he being the husband or father he should be. But the draw of the flesh was strong, feeding all those feelings he had harbored within himself for years.

Sin always pays a price. Sinners always get caught. Someone always finds out. And that was true for John. One day his adultery with this woman was discovered and his pastor called him into his office. That's the last place John wanted to be.

The pastor and associate pastor confronted John, and he admitted his adultery. The pastor began to work with him but never made John's sin public. In fact, no one ever told Maggie. John was counseled but not disciplined, helped but not cured. "This, I believe, was a part of the problem," John admitted. "I realized I could continue to sin; and even if I got caught, nothing really would happen."

Déjà Vu, All Over Again

For the next four or five years, John lived as straight as an arrow, but not without testing his character. His job took him out of town constantly, and the lure of sin was always there. In fact, opportunities to sin were almost constant. Unless John had gotten ahold of his pride, his ego and his penchant for using people for his own purposes, it was just a matter of time until opportunity met desire.

John remembers, "Since I continued to live a life of performance-based Christianity, it didn't take long for those feelings of wanting to be found attractive, fun and successful to begin to replace any feelings I had of wanting to be obedient and faithful to my Heavenly Father." John's spirit may have been willing but his flesh was definitely weak. Being strong and athletic are no safeguards against being weak in the flesh.

Soon John was up to his old tricks. There were numerous new affairs. Most of them were of the one or two-night type. Others lasted for a number of months. John was digging a deeper pit for himself every time he slept with another woman. He said sadly, "Some of these women I didn't even know their names. Most of them I didn't care to know. I was so used to using other people that I treated them as throwaways."

Often John questioned his salvation. "How could a Christian repeatedly be involved in adulterous relationships like this?" he would ask himself. A tremendous conflict arose between knowing what was right and holy as opposed to the overwhelming pull of his flesh. That pull of the flesh was dominating his life. He was not in control anymore, and the Spirit of God was certainly not in control either. "I pleaded with God to make me stop. But I never had the godly character to flee the temptation or stop myself."

John knew he had to make a change in his life. Unfortunately, he tried to make that change without adequately dealing with his sin. Instead, he sought out a change of employment, something that would allow him more time at home and less time to be tempted by so many women.

New Opportunities

God opened the door. John became the general manager of a Christian bookstore in his hometown. He loved the protective environment a Christian business provided. But he still found the need to perform, to be seen by others as successful. And John was successful. He built that business into one of the largest of its kind in the country. He even served on the board of directors of the association that serves Christian bookstores. He was seen in the industry as one of the brightest and best, and that's what he wanted. What he didn't want is what happened next.

Because John had never adequately dealt with his past sins but simply covered over them, he was not prepared to deal with similar kinds of sin now. He was living a double life: a successful Christian businessman and a thirsty sinner at the same time.

In his own words, John relates what happened next. "Pride raised its ugly head and I found myself in a counseling situation with one of the young female employees at the store. It didn't take long for me once again to jump into an immoral and devastating affair. I had many before, but this time my plan was to walk away from everything and begin a new life with this young woman. I was sure this would satisfy those dark longings of my heart and give me a real pride ride."

John's latest affair lasted nearly three years. It ended up costing him his business and his position on the board of directors; and had it not been for God's grace and a godly wife, it would have cost him Maggie too.

Free at Last

There would be no sweeping this round of sin under the rug like so many rounds before it. John was placed under church discipline, and that was the best thing for him. John had fooled everyone, including himself. He admits, "At that point, everyone could finally see me for who I really was. All my performance, all the careful planning of how to have my sinful needs met, all the pride that surrounded my life—it was all stripped away. I was humiliated before my church, my friends and my family. But for the first time in my life, I was free from the need for performance and people pleasing. For the first time in my life, it wasn't about me!"

John's days of living two lives were over. His humiliation was ultimately the key to unlocking his prison's door. God had lovingly but firmly taken John McNally to the end of himself so he could be delivered from the bondage to himself.

The spiritual issues in John's life were resolved through the process of repentance and restoration. That was the easy part. The practical part of restoration would take much longer.

John is especially grateful for two people in his life: his pastor, who lovingly walked him through the process of repentance and restoration, monitoring his progress all the way; and especially for Maggie, his wife. Throughout John's life, Maggie was the one he had hurt the most. Still, she faithfully and unconditionally loved him for over 30 years, and John knew that relationship needed some immediate and significant repair.

Always, There Was Maggie

The bond of trust that plays so critical a role in a marriage relationship was badly damaged by John over, and over, and over again. John knew he was going to have to earn Maggie's trust, and to earn it every day (and night) of his life. They are working at it now. John thanks God every day that, in spite of his repeated and blatant sin, Maggie stood by him and that God is restoring their marriage, not to what it was before but to what it was meant to be from the beginning.

But adultery hurts everyone—the Savior, the church, the friends, the spouse, and the family. Being restored to his children and grandchildren was equally difficult for John. He admits, "To be known as a man without godly character has been excruciating for me. I finally realized that I could no longer just say the right words and things would be okay. My life so desperately needed to reflect and validate those words. That process continues to this day. I am determined to finish strong and to provide my family with the godly leadership and example they have deserved all their lives but I have failed to provide."

Lessons Learned

Both John and Maggie learned a great deal through these harrowing years—about themselves and about each other. But since this book is about surviving the prodigals in your life, let's hear from Maggie.

"When I first found out about John's adultery," Maggie remembers, "I didn't know what to do. I couldn't believe it. I wanted to believe it wasn't true, but I knew it was." Often Maggie would get alone with God and simply talk to Him. "I remember one time at Tucker Lake, walking along the lake, weeping before God and pouring out my heart, my hurt and my rejection. I genuinely felt His presence walking with me. He impressed upon me that He, too, was rejected without cause, and it was as if He carried me along that day."

And what has Maggie learned through her ordeal with a prodigal spouse? Two things specifically.

First, "I began dating John when I was 16 years old. I was young and John was my life. Now as I have grown in spiritual maturity, I realize that it was a mistake to idolize the man who would become my husband. I had put him before the Lord Jesus in my life, and that was a costly mistake. Now I know that it is in Jesus that 'we live and move and have our being' (Acts 17:28), not in any other person. Never again will a man be my all in all. John is a part of my life again, but we build our lives on Christ alone." An important lesson for all of us.

Second, Maggie says, "After reading Henri Nouwen's book *Return of the Prodigal Son*, I have found that I, too, am a prodigal. I am the elder brother and am fighting to this day self-righteousness, self-pity, depression, isolation and bitterness. I have the same choice as John had—to choose to respond to him in God's way or to respond to my repentant husband in my way. If I am unforgiving, unbending now, he will no longer be the prodigal spouse in our family; I will be."

There are potentially two prodigals in every story. One may begin as the runaway, but the other can end up as the castaway. Maggie knew that when John was broken because of his sin, the only way for her to have victory was to keep from being the older brother in Jesus' parable.

Hope for a Persistent Prodigal

During his many forays into sin, and even during the days of being restored to the life of the family, John often questioned whether or not his salvation was real. "I know now that it was," John says. "I also know that even a saved person can be so caught in the bondage of sin that we often appear to be no different than an unbeliever." The deception of sin is real and the pull of the flesh is like a strong magnet. We all must be bathed daily in the power of the Holy Spirit and spend significant time in God's Word if we want to escape the lust of the flesh.

So what would Maggie say to anyone who has been the victim of a prodigal spouse? "You must learn to rely on God's faithfulness, even if you couldn't rely on your husband's faithfulness. 'My Redeemer is faithful and true' almost became a mantra to me during those dark days. One verse that got me through John's unfaithfulness was Isaiah 30:15. I claimed the first part for John, and the second part for me. 'In returning and rest you shall be saved; in quietness and confidence shall be your strength'" (NKJV).

And what would John say to anyone who has engaged in a prodigal lifestyle as he has? Simply this: "I am convinced that the only hope for a prodigal like me is the supernatural intervention of God. Otherwise, the bondage and deception will continue. I am so thankful for that day more than four years ago when God intervened, exposed me for the prodigal I was and brought me home again. There is nothing, absolutely nothing, that satisfies like being pure, clean and holy before the Lord. Nothing!"

John and Maggie McNally's story is a story of beauty from ashes. It's the kind of story repeated over and over when prodigals remember their Father and act in ways that give Him pleasure and give them victory.

Part Four

SURVIVING LIFE'S PRODIGALS
How to Cope With the Prodigals in Your Life

Chapter 15

FIRST STEPS TO SURVIVAL

"Do what you can; let God do the rest"

You've gone out to eat for the evening. At the restaurant the server has taken your order but your food hasn't arrived yet. Killing time you casually glance around the room.

Suddenly, at a table near you, you spy a man choking on his food. No one else notices him so you rush over and perform the Heimlich maneuver on him. His food is dislodged and he begins to breathe. You're an instant hero. It was the right first response.

You're sitting on a park bench watching your children enjoy the playground. They like the slides and the merry-go-round, but especially the swings. Your little six-year-old is swinging higher and higher. You warn her but she doesn't stop. Suddenly she falls from the swing and lies unconscious in the dust. Someone quickly dials 911 and an ambulance is there in minutes. It was the right first response.

First Things First

Doing the right things first can be the difference between life and death. That's true when it comes to our wayward children, spouses or church members. Doing the right things first can make the difference between surviving a prodigal or not.

When Jesus told the parable of the lost son, He told it as the third in a trilogy of stories. First there was the story of the lost sheep. Then the lost coin. Finally the lost son.

In the first story, the shepherd placed 99 sheep in a safe place while he went out after the one lost sheep. In the second story, the woman placed nine coins in a safe place while she swept the house, looking for the one lost coin. But in the story of the prodigal son, the father didn't go after his son. He stayed at home and waited for him to return. Have you ever wondered why?

Perhaps Jesus wanted us to learn the first things we should do when our situation appears to be hopeless. Maybe He wanted to give us the first steps to take when we're attempting to survive the prodigals in our life.

When you don't know what to do, what do you do first? The parable of the prodigal son reflects some initial responses. Think of them as the first steps to survival. And put them into practice when you have a prodigal in your life.

Go After a Prodigal If You Can

In the story of the lost sheep, that one straying lamb couldn't have gone very far. Where could he go? In the wilderness there aren't that many places to hide. He could wander into a ravine, hide out in a cave, maybe get his wool caught in a nearby thicket. A wandering sheep didn't have many options in Palestine.

In the story of the lost coin, the money was contained within the confines of the woman's house. Where could it go? It could roll under the floor mat she used as a bed. It could find a tiny crevice in the dirt floor. It could hide in a dark corner. But it couldn't get far. It remained within her small house.

But the parable of the lost son is vastly different. The prodigal had a whole world in which to lose himself. He wasn't wedged in a nearby crag or lost in his father's house. He traveled to a distant country and nobody knew where. The prodigal left no forwarding address; he never wrote home. The father had no idea where the son went. How could he possibly go after him?

If you know where your prodigal is holed up, if you can trace where he or she is living, don't sit back and wait for that prodigal to come home. You only prolong his or her agony, and yours. Go after your prodigal. Seek him or her out. Find out where he or she is staying and extend the invitation to come home again. Enjoy forgiveness.

If the father could have gone after his son to retrieve him, you know he would have done so. But he couldn't; he didn't know where his prodigal was. If you know where yours is, do what the shepherd did. Go after your lost sheep. Do what the woman did. Sweep the area to find your lost coin. If you can, go after your prodigal and plead with him or her to return.

Wait Patiently for Your Prodigal

The father knew his son's need, but he had no way of finding him. The inability to go after his son drove the father to the only thing he could do. He waited—patiently, longingly, prayerfully.

We've already talked about waiting. Nobody likes to do it, but sometimes that's all you can do. Fortunately, when you're praying for a prodigal spouse or a prodigal son or daughter to return, you don't have to wait in a coma. There are things you can do while you wait. The father in Jesus' family portrait did them; so can you.

While waiting, the father scanned the horizon in expectation. He was looking for someone very dear to him. He scanned the fields for his son as an air traffic controller scans his radar screen looking for a lost airplane. He waited. He watched. He prayed. And one day, one glorious day, he rejoiced.

If your only recourse is to wait for your prodigal to return home, take special note of how the father waited. He went on with his normal life. He had a house to keep, a farm to run, another son to love, servants to feed and care for. He had a life to live. His heart was broken, but life had to go on. Others depended on him.

Still, his prodigal was never out of his mind. The one straying sheep was never out of the shepherd's mind until he found it. That one lost coin troubled the woman until she found it. Your prodigal will weigh heavily on your mind; you can count on it. So ask God to give you the proper balance of caring for the 99 and the one. Ask Him to let you scan the horizon and look after the needs of your family at the same time. He'll help you; He's just that kind of God.

Give Your Anxiety to God

In your attempt to survive the prodigals in your life, one thing is certain—you're going to be filled with anxiety about them. You wouldn't be human if you weren't.

But God's Word has some sound advice for you. David had a few prodigal sons of his own. Still he could counsel us, "Commit your way to the LORD; trust in him and he will do this.... Be still before the LORD and wait patiently for him....Do not fret—it leads only to evil" (Ps. 37:5,7-8).

Did you notice the verbs? Commit. Trust. Be still. Wait patiently. Do not fret. A pretty tall order when your life is falling apart. But we have a pretty big God. He can bring peace in the midst of your storm. God can bring quiet order to the noisy chaos of your life. He can bring rest when your mind is racing a hundred miles an hour.

Peter gave us similar advice. Speaking of Jesus, he said, "Cast all your anxiety on him because he cares for you" (1 Pet. 5:7).

Have you tried that yet? Have you tried unloading the burden of your prodigal on the Lord Jesus? Have you asked Him to share your burden? Or do you prefer to shoulder that burden all alone? When it comes to anxiety, you can cast or you can keep. The choice is yours. Which will it be?

Don't Forget to Pray

Here's another first step to survival. When someone dear to you has wandered away from the faith, when your child has left home and is living in the world, it's normal to be filled with anxiety, but it's neither healthy nor helpful. Anxiety contributes to a host of physical and spiritual maladies. Besides, being anxious doesn't help bring your prodigal back anyway.

So what does help? Do what the father in this parable did. "Do not be anxious about anything, but in everything, by prayer and petition, with thanksgiving, present your requests to God. And the peace of God, which transcends all understanding, will guard your hearts and your minds in Christ Jesus" (Phil. 4:6-7). That's a formula for serenity, for sleep, for success!

Remember what the old hymn says? "O what peace we often forfeit, O what needless pain we bear, all because we do not carry, everything to God in prayer."

Don't let a day go by that you fail to commit your prodigals to the Lord in prayer. Ask God to bring them to their senses. Ask Him to protect them from danger and bring them home again. Perhaps your prodigals are still at home and yet live in a distant land of sin. Ask God to convict them of sin and draw them to Himself. Pray every day that God will do His wondrous work of grace in their hearts. Regardless of the circumstances, only God can bring a prodigal home again or replenish the joy of those who never left home.

Never Give Up Hope

Don't be filled with apprehension and anxiety. Don't be filled with anger and frustration. Don't be filled with guilt and shame. Instead, keep your prodigal before the Lord in consistent prayer. The prayers of concerned and compassionate parents will do more to bring a prodigal back than anything else. Pray daily for your prodigal.

But do more than that. Expect God to bring them back. It may be soon or it may be awhile, but expect God to bring your prodigal home again.

The father in Jesus' story would not have scanned the horizon daily had he not expected God would bring his son home. He wanted the son back, he prayed for his return, and he expected it.

But what if your prodigal doesn't soon return? What if you've prayed and waited, but he or she isn't back? Don't give up hope. Never stop praying and anticipating. Awaken each morning in anticipation that this will be the day you see your prodigal come home again. As long as prodigals are alive, there's reason to have hope.

Hope is not something we do; hope is something we have. Of the 87 times the Greek word for *hope* occurs in the New Testament, 61 percent of those times it is used as a noun. Hope is something concrete. It's something you hang onto. Have hope that your prodigal will return. Grab that hope and hang onto it.

There may not be many things you can do to bring your prodigal back, but the initial things you do are the most crucial things. It's like performing the Heimlich maneuver or dialing 911. They are the right first steps, and that's important if you are to survive the prodigals in your life.

Chapter 16

SURVIVING A PRODIGAL SPOUSE

"Do the responsible thing"

Perhaps the most painful form of prodigalism is not a wayward son or daughter, but rather a wayward spouse. If you are the victim of a runaway spouse, there's something for you in Jesus' story of the father trapped between two prodigals. You can survive a prodigal spouse, and here's how.

Commensurate with the decay of biblical morality in America (and the rest of the world), has been the rise in adult prodigalism. More and more adults are simply walking away from their responsibilities. They're seeking more exciting, more meaningful lives. Nowhere is this tragedy more evident than in the marriage relationship.

Estimates vary according to the population surveyed, but respected sociologist Laurel Richardson has determined that 40-50 percent of married American males have been unfaithful to their wives. About 15 percent of the married population has been repeatedly unfaithful.[1] This means they have been involved in a series of adulterous relationships.

Think of it this way. In our quiet suburban developments, perhaps like the area in which you live, nearly every other house has a prodigal spouse. In our urban apartment complexes teeming with people, nearly every other apartment is inhabited by a prodigal spouse.

It was noted earlier that runaway teens do not come predominantly from poor or underprivileged families. Likewise the prodigal spouse is more apt to come from upper-income groups. The incidence of adultery in men rises to 70 percent for those men earning in excess of $60,000 annually.

So let's put to rest all our fanciful excuses for prodigalism. Prodigalism in adults usually is not due to abuse. It's not the result of boredom. Prodigalism is the result of sin, just plain old-fashioned sin! Prodigal adults are sinning adults, not just consenting adults. The root of prodigalism is sin.

Behaving Like a Prodigal Spouse

Gus is a good example of a prodigal adult. Born in Africa, Gus was the son of a passive father and a dominant mother. His home life created deep bitterness in Gus' heart. He developed a rebellious nature. During his teen years Gus drew trouble like a powerful magnet.

Gus became a promiscuous rebel, losing his virginity at age 16. By his own admission, he enjoyed sin solely because it was sin. Gus looked for any and all forms of sin he could find.

As a young adult Gus shared an apartment with a live-in girl-friend. Later she bore his son. Like many prodigal spouses, Gus grew tired of their relationship. He was self-absorbed and irresponsible. He abandoned both the woman and his son and left home, much like the prodigal in Jesus' story.

Gus had a hard time finding himself. He went to Europe and studied philosophy but found no peace in education. He dabbled in astrology but found no guidance there. It was not until age 37 that Gus realized what his problem was—he needed God and he needed to be more responsible to those whose lives he had shattered. Finally Gus fell to his knees and trusted Jesus Christ as his Savior.

Elsewhere in this book I have not used the real names of people mentioned, but in Gus' case you've probably already made a positive identification. Gus is short for Augustine, one of the greatest of the church fathers.

In the fourth century Augustine was a prodigal spouse, even though he hadn't married the woman he lived with. He just walked away from their relationship, leaving mother and child and all his responsibilities behind. Sin does that to a person.

Just Plain Sin

Sometimes a man moves out of the house due to anger. Unresolved tension in the home drives a husband to seek a quieter haven with someone else. Some unfaithful spouses have understandable reasons for their emotions, but not for their sin. It's a fallacy that adultery is a man's way of relieving his anger. It's simply a way of satisfying his lust.

Frequently a wife becomes adulterous because of desperate loneliness. She no longer feels needed by her husband. Their marriage relationship is platonic. They only stay together for the children or for window dressing. She's at home and extremely lonely. She wanders into prodigalism, looking for love in all the wrong places. But her wandering is still sin. Adultery is never justified in God's eyes.

Some spouses have a craving for freedom the way the prodigal son did. Their spouse seems too possessive of them, too domineering. They just want to get away, to take control of their own situation, to run their own life. They exhibit a great number of the symptoms exhibited by the prodigal in Jesus' parable. They wander away from their family out of self-indulgence, self-preoccupation, self-gratification. But their wandering is self-defeating because it is sinful. They'll find themselves with nothing but the pods to be fed to the pigs.

Do the Responsible Thing

Have you become a prodigal spouse? If so, what must you do to enable your spouse to survive? Perhaps you're still living at home, but you're living a lie. You're a prodigal and you know it. Even at home you're living in "a distant country." How can you ever make things right?

Jesus' five steps to reconciliation are set in concrete. It's the kind of concrete that both restores marriages and then holds them together. That's what prodigal spouses need just as much as prodigal sons.

If you're a prodigal spouse, first realize that the responsibility to make things right is yours. Don't rationalize your motives for leaving home; just go back home. Take the personal action the prodigal son took. You've got to go home to make things right. That's where the trouble began; that's where it must end. It's the only way.

Once home you'll face a personal confrontation with your spouse. You may want to seek the help of someone on your pastoral staff or a spiritual counselor. Find someone who can cut through all the psychological jargon and get to God's solution. If your pastor cannot help you, ask him to refer you to someone who can. The confrontation involves your spouse and you, but it's best accomplished with a spiritually qualified helper in your presence.

Speak to your spouse directly, kindly. The prodigal son confessed to his father, and that was hard. You must address your repentance to the one you previously addressed your anger to—the one you love and have hurt the most. Make your confession personal. Make it real. Make it sincere. Don't quibble about the circumstances that led you to become a prodigal spouse. Confess your sin for what it really is—sin.

Responding to a Prodigal Spouse

But what if you're not the prodigal spouse? What if you're the one who has been hurt, the one left at home, the one humiliated by the prodigal behavior of your spouse? What should you do? How should a faithful spouse respond to a prodigal?

Perhaps your spouse has remarried and there is no road back. The road is closed. It will never reopen. Accept that and go on with your life. But if the road remains open, however rocky it may be, there are things you can do.

The basic biblical principle is this: If you have been hurt by a prodigal spouse, respond the same way the father responded to his lost son. Respond the way the woman responded to her lost coin. Respond the way the shepherd responded to his lost sheep. If there are steps you can take to retrieve your prodigal, take those steps. The shepherd did. The woman did. If there don't seem to be any steps you can take, do what the father did. Pray that person back. Ask God to convict your prodigal of his or her foolishness and bring him or her back to you. Make their return a matter of fervent, daily prayer.

But do more than that. Scan the horizon. Expect God to bring your spouse back. Cling to genuine hope. In society today, our expectations are just the opposite. We expect once a spouse is gone, that wife or husband will be gone forever. But God is the God of the second chance. He is the God of restoration. He is the God of real hope. He is the God of the impossible. Expect Him to do the impossible. Expect Him to bring your prodigal spouse home again.

Don't Forget to Forgive

And when God does bring your spouse home, be sure to receive your prodigal in the way the father received his. It's not easy to be compassionate when you've been hurt. It's not easy to forgive when you've been wronged. In fact, it's not natural. It's supernatural. Ask God to give you supernatural grace—grace greater than all your spouse's sin. Ask Him to give you the kind of forgiving spirit the father had in Jesus' story, the kind our Heavenly Father has.

Jesus taught His followers, "For if you forgive men when they sin against you, your heavenly Father will also forgive you. But if you do not forgive men their sins, your Father will not forgive your sins" (Matt. 6:14-15). Wounded spouse, your Father in heaven has forgiven your trespasses; it looks like it's your turn.

Hanging there on the cross, after they had mocked Him, spat upon Him, and crowned Him with thorns, Jesus cried out, "Father, forgive them." He didn't say this because these prodigals were innocent but because they were guilty. You don't need to forgive the innocent. Forgive your husband because he is guilty, not because he is innocent. Jesus did not forgive these prodigals because they were deserving but because He was forgiving. Forgive your wife because you are forgiving, not because she is deserving.

Desires and Dilemmas

Forgiveness is the desire of every repentant prodigal. It's the dilemma of every responsible spouse. Should you forgive or not? Should you punish or not? Should you restore your prodigal spouse or not?

These questions never entered the father's mind in Jesus' story. He told this parable so we would know how to relate to one another. The way the father related to his prodigal is the way God wants us to relate to our prodigals, even if we are married to them.

When asking yourself how to return if you're a prodigal or how to respond to your returning prodigal, don't allow the lessons of this parable to slip your attention. They provide God's program for coming home again and being graciously received.

You can survive a prodigal spouse but only if you survive the way the father survived in Jesus' story. Survive through compassion. Survive through forgiveness. Survive through reclaiming all that is good in your spouse rather than reliving all that is bad.

You can survive, but survival is up to you. It's your choice. Choose survival and move on with your life for God.

Notes

1. Laurel Richardson, *The New Other Woman* (New York: The Free Press, 1985), 1.

Chapter 17

SURVIVING OLDER BROTHERS

"Am I an older brother?"

Surviving an older brother requires a slightly different approach than surviving a prodigal child or spouse. But Jesus included the older brother in His parable to demonstrate that you don't have to leave home to be a prodigal.

Since *prodigal* means "extravagant or wasteful," it's legitimate to ask how the older brother was a prodigal. As the story unfolds, it becomes painfully evident that the older brother wasted his years as did his young sibling. He faithfully worked for his father, but because of his faulty attitudes toward his father, all those years were wasted. These attitudes boiled beneath the surface and erupted only when the younger son returned home.

While the younger son was a prodigal in body, the older son was a prodigal in heart. He was in the field working, but his heart wasn't in his work. He was only going through the motions. Strange, isn't it? While the prodigal son's hands were busy feeding the pigs, his heart was at home. But while the older son's hands were busy at home, his heart was miles away.

This older brother did exhibit some very commendable virtues. No one could say he wasn't faithful. No one could criticize his work. He always obeyed the father. He never brought disgrace to his family name. He was obedient to the commands of the Law and undoubtedly kept most of them. What a guy!

But he kept the Law the same way the Pharisees kept it—by letter, not by spirit. He kept the statutes of the Law, but he despised his brother who broke them. As the prodigal son represents those who have lived far from God's standard, the older brother represents those who have lived within it but have maintained a heart attitude that was far from it.

Surviving Older Brothers

So you've got some older brothers in your church. How are you to live with them? How will you survive them? Jesus' parable has the answer. If you treat the crabgrass kids in your church the way the father treated the older brother in Jesus' parable, you can survive them. Let's see how.

It's evident this father loved both his sons—the younger prodigal and the older prodigal. He loved them dearly. He loved them equally. He treated them as evenhandedly as he loved them.

But what makes this father's evenhanded treatment so evident? If we comb the parable, especially the father's final response, we'll discover some clues to properly responding to all the prodigals in your life.

CLUE 1—*The father treated both sons fairly.*

When the older brother complained about the big to-do over the prodigal, the father replied, "You are always with me, and everything I have is yours (v. 31)."

The boy was always there. He never left. His father recognized that. But he also recognized that his older son had received the double portion of the inheritance. All of that was still his.

But now the prodigal was back, and the older brother didn't want him back. What was the problem? Maybe he was concerned the father would again divide the family inheritance. Would the prodigal son receive another share? Would this mean less for the older brother?

Not at all. The father already gave the younger son his share of the estate and he squandered it; it was gone forever. It would not be replaced, even though the son was received back into the family.

What the older brother did not see in his jealous rage was that nothing materially had changed when his brother came home again. The father's words "Everything I have is yours" reaffirmed that he would not renege on allowing the elder son to keep his inheritance.

The father had treated his runaway son fairly. The son had acted foolishly; and though repentant and returned, foolishness always pays a heavy wage. Some live foolishly and lose their money. Some live foolishly and lose their virginity. Some live foolishly and lose their health. Just because our foolish living is forgiven doesn't mean all we've lost is restored.

On the other hand, the older brother was also treated fairly. His inheritance was intact. It belonged to him before the younger son left home. It was his the whole time the prodigal was gone. And it remained his now that the younger son had come home again.

The father dealt fairly with both his sons, according to the law. His righteous character would permit him to do no less. That's how to survive older brothers. Treat them as fairly as you treat other prodigals. Don't permit the return of a prodigal to your church to go by unnoticed; but don't permit the faithfulness of an older brother to go by unrewarded. Be fair to both and survive.

CLUE 2—The father treated both sons tenderly.

It's possible to be fair and yet so businesslike that you lack the compassion of God. The father was both fair and tender.

When he responded to the older brother's ugly anger, the father called him "son." True, the older brother was his son; the father had every reason to call him that. But what he actually said was even more intimate.

Jesus had several words in His vocabulary that He could have placed on the father's tongue in this story. He did not choose the Greek word *huios*—the normal word for "son, a male offspring." Instead He chose the word *teknon*, which means "child," not "son." *Teknon* is an expression of extreme tenderness, the kind of tenderness older brothers need if they're to survive in the church.

When the father referred to his son as child, he was not implying childish behavior, even though the older brother behaved childishly. He wanted to express the genuineness of his relationship with his son. *Teknon* was used when you referred to a true, genuine child as opposed to someone who bore no relationship to you. He was his flesh and blood, no less important to the father than his younger son was.

The same is true for us. All who know Christ as Savior are the children of God. We are genuine heirs of God and joint-heirs with Christ Jesus (Rom. 8:17). We are not just offspring; we are His flesh and blood.

But sometimes—like older brothers—we act more like children than grown-ups. Paul expressed his dismay at the Corinthian believers because their petty differences made them act like spiritual babies (1 Cor. 3:1-7). Our Heavenly Father does the same with us. If we have been born again (John 3:1-7), we are the genuine children of God. As His children, when we do not act our age spiritually, God must chide us. He does it tenderly, however, and with genuine care for us. He's just that kind of God.

When you must confront an older brother in your congregation who is acting a bit childish over the return of a prodigal, do so with tenderness. Remember, older brothers are as much a part of the family as the prodigal is—no less, no more. Their response to the prodigal's return may be wrong, but even older brothers need the tenderness of God when you deal with them.

CLUE 3—*The father treated both sons equally.*

There are remarkable parallels in Jesus' parable to the way the father treated his sons. For example, when the younger son demanded his inheritance, the father divided the inheritance between both sons. Although the older brother demanded nothing, the father treated his sons equally.

Throughout the journey home the beleaguered prodigal must have wondered whether his father would receive him back. Would he even answer his knock at the door? As it turns out, the son had nothing to worry about. He never had a chance to knock. The father ran out of the house to meet him. The father came to him.

This detail we rarely miss. The father came out of the house to get the prodigal son. But there's a similar detail in Jesus' story that we almost always miss. When the older brother heard music and dancing and was so angered he would not enter the house, what did the father do? Verse 28 says, "So his father went out and pleaded with him." The father came out of the house to meet the older brother. The father begged him to return home again. Exactly what he did for his other prodigal son.

These sons were treated equally by the father. There was no distinction in his efforts to salvage them. He loved them both. He came to them both. He entreated them both. One of the prodigals heeded that entreaty and came home again. We don't know about the second one.

If you want to survive the older brothers in your life, treat them as treasures. Don't take them for granted. Be lavish in your prayers and praises for them. Show them you care. And if they begin acting like an older brother when a prodigal returns, survive them the way the father survived his stay-at-home prodigal. Treat them fairly, treat them tenderly, treat them equally.

CLUE 4—The father treated both sons individually.

Did the father in the parable know his sons? Did he know their strengths and weaknesses, their foibles, their idiosyncrasies? You know he did. After all, he didn't have ten sons; he only had two. He knew they were different, very different from each other. He knew their temperaments. He was a compassionate father. He knew them.

And when each disappointed him, he treated his sons individually. He ministered to the broken heart of the runaway son. And he ministered to the bruised psyche of the older brother. Their needs were different and individual, and the father met them differently and individually

In our cold and impersonal world, we rarely treat people as individuals anymore. There are only two occasions when our name is sure to appear in the local newspaper—the day we are born and the day we die. In between we are "society."

In the introduction to this book, I noted that when the judge enters the courtroom, we hear, "All rise!" When the lecture is over, the professor says, "Class dismissed." Individuals in the same church congregation are "members." It's hard to be treated as an individual in our burgeoning population.

But the father treated his sons individually. He met the needs of the younger son with individual attention. And he met the needs of the older brother with individual attention. Nowhere in the story is this more evident than in the last verse: "But we had to celebrate and be glad, because this brother of yours was dead and is alive again; he was lost and is found."

The need of the runaway son was for acceptance and forgiveness. That's why the father did not back down when the older brother griped about the party for the younger son. It was the appropriate thing for the father to do. It was an individual act of healing.

The need of the older brother was also for acceptance and forgiveness, but with a significant difference. While the younger brother needed to be accepted and forgiven, the older brother needed to be accepting and forgiving. Jesus never indicated that the older brother was. As the story ends, the father is pleading with him to be forgiving.

Still, we dare not miss the individual healing offered by the father. While the older brother would only refer to the prodigal as "this son of yours" (v. 30) and not "my brother," notice the father does not refer to the prodigal as "this son of mine," but rather "this brother of yours" (v. 32). What a classic example of the psychology of hurt being met by the psychology of healing.

It's Your Turn

Was the father in Jesus' story a master psychologist? Was he a brilliant strategist? Maybe, but more than anything, he was what the two prodigals needed—a compassionate, concerned, caring father. He was deeply loving to both his sons, even though he was deeply hurt by both.

Now it's your turn. Older brothers in your local assembly need tenderly to be reminded that prodigals are not just "God's children" but also "brothers and sisters." We have a relationship with God and therefore with each other. You can survive the prodigals in your church only if you help them recover and be restored.

Emphasize your family relationship with returned prodigals. Create social situations in which you can foster that relationship. Help these older brothers to get to know their siblings as well as the Father does. That's the only way they'll be as compassionate toward them as He was.

"Blessed are the peacemakers, for they will be called sons of God" (Matt. 5:9). Ironic, isn't it, that this is the only one of Jesus' Beatitudes that emphasizes our family relationship.

Be a peacemaker at church. Put your arm around the older brothers and be a peacemaker for them. Be a survivor by making them survivors too.

Chapter 18

THE BOTTOM-LINE QUESTION

"Who was hurt the most?"

Have you noticed how often parents find themselves in the middle of an argument—not between themselves but between their children? If you're a mom or dad, you know exactly what I'm talking about.

Two sisters fall in love with the guy who moved in next door. Dad and Mom find themselves in the role of United Nations negotiators. Two brothers pool their resources to buy an old car. But when a new engine is needed, one brother is mysteriously broke. Dad and Mom have to intervene. Add your own horror story here.

Frequently parents are caught in the middle. Their children won't speak to each other, so the parents must speak for them. It's like sitting on a stone wall, speaking to a son on one side of the wall and then relaying the message to the son on the other side. Maybe you've been there.

In Jesus' story the younger prodigal interfaced with the father, and the older prodigal interfaced with the father. But the two brothers never interfaced with each other. Nowhere in the parable did they speak to each other. Nowhere did they even look one another in the eye, face-to-face. Their only contact was through a third party—the father.

Trouble in the Church Family

What happens at home sometimes happens in the church as well. I have preached in churches where upon entering the sanctuary I sensed the presence of the Hatfields and McCoys. Members of the church family had been at odds with one another for years. They would carefully plan their activities, carefully time their arrivals and departures, even carefully gauge where they sat in order to avoid

171

talking with each other. Caught in the middle was the pastor and maybe some of the elders. The whole church was hamstrung because of the immaturity of these family members.

But there's a problem with being in the middle. Sometimes you get hurt. When you're assaulted broadside, at least you can muster your defenses and concentrate at the point of attack. But what about being assaulted from two sides? What happens when you're caught in the middle?

Everyone in Jesus' parable experienced a great deal of pain. No one was exempt—because it was a family in pain. The prodigal son experienced the pain of humiliation. The father experienced the pain of rejection. The older brother experienced the pain of bitterness. But while each one experienced pain, the pain of one must have been excruciating.

Getting to the Bottom Line

There are many questions in this parable that beg answers. But one question towers above the others. It is this. In this parable of the prodigal, the father and the older brother, which one was hurt the most? Which one had to endure the greatest pain?

At first glance, you may think the prodigal was hurt the most. After all, only he experienced the famine. Only he suffered the humiliation of feeding the pigs. Only he had to come crawling back to the family. The prodigal son must have experienced the greatest pain. Surely he was hurt the most.

But the prodigal son was the only one who traveled to a distant land. He was the only one who saw the world. The prodigal was the only one who lived it up. And the prodigal finally experienced the joy of forgiveness when he returned to the life of the family. We have no evidence the older brother ever enjoyed these things.

Perhaps it was the older brother who experienced the greatest hurt. After all, he remained behind and worked diligently for the father. No party was ever thrown in his honor. No one ever patted him on the back or even said thank you. He experienced the pain of being taken for granted. Surely he was hurt the most.

But the older brother was never hungry. He never experienced famine. He was never so desperate that he craved carob pods. He was saved the ethnic humiliation of feeding the pigs. He never knew what it was to be penniless, homeless, friendless.

No, the younger brother was not hurt the most, but neither was the older brother. So who was hurt the most?

The Father Was Hurt the Most

I think the person hurt the most in Jesus' parable was the father. That's ironic, too, because he was the one who loved the most. He was hurt by the words and actions of both sons. He was hurt from two directions, not just one. He was in the middle, the place of greatest danger when the hurt began to fly.

The father was hurt by the insensitivity of the prodigal son. He was hurt by the boy's unreasonable demand. He was hurt by his son's lack of respect. He must have been crushed when the boy left home, proving he preferred the father's money to the father's love.

But the father was also hurt by the malignancy of the older brother. He was hurt by his implacable hatred. He was hurt by his son's lack of compassion. He must have been crushed when this boy lashed out at him angrily, proving he preferred the father's celebration to the father's love.

A Tale of Two Brothers

Let me tell you the story of two brothers, both of whom owned bicycles. Since I mentioned earlier that I have an older brother and had a bicycle as a boy, let me hasten to add that this is not a personal story.

Once there were two brothers. Each had a bicycle. The day came when the younger boy took a pair of tin snips and cut all the spokes in his brother's bicycle. The older brother couldn't let something like that happen without retaliation, so he took those same tin snips and cut the spokes in his brother's bicycle.

Question. Who was hurt the most? Answer. The father. He had to buy two new bicycles.

In Jesus' beautiful family portrait, each brother was hurt by the other, but the father was hurt the most. It's always that way.

It's that way in the church family. When there is a spat between two people in church, when you and another Christian aren't getting along, when there is resentment and jealousy in the family, when one church is fighting with another church, when one Christian is suing another Christian—when these things happen, both family members are hurt, but our Heavenly Father is always hurt the most.

When we hurt ourselves, we hurt our Heavenly Father. When we hurt others, we hurt our Heavenly Father. If we learn anything from this parable, we must learn that the father is always hurt the most.

To be less like the prodigal sons and more like the father, resolve never to stray from the life of the family. Resolve to nip prodigalism in the bud before a treasured brother or sister wanders from the church family. But resolve with equal determination never to become an older brother yourself.

Do whatever it takes, endure whatever it takes, to be congenial and compassionate in both your home and church families. Be less critical, less caustic, less like the older brother and more like the father. Clip the wings of Pharisaism before your son or daughter runs from home or a treasured brother or sister becomes bitter and takes flight from the church family.

You can survive a prodigal in your life. The father in Jesus' parable survived two of them. But to survive your prodigal you must live so that you guard against hurting the Father. That's the best way to avoid becoming either a prodigal son or an older brother yourself.

FAMILY BETRAYAL

George and Katie Sandt

Some stories of prodigals have to be true. When you hear them, you know they are real; you couldn't make up a story like that. The story you are about to read is one of those real stories of prodigals.

George and Katie Sandt were a young Christian couple, expecting their first child. Those were exciting days. God had brought them together and now He was giving them the gift of a little baby.

But just hours before Katie was to deliver, the doctor said, "I'm deeply concerned about your baby, Mrs. Sandt. I don't detect any heartbeat." The young couple were devastated, and as they held each other in their arms all they could do was pray.

"Dear Father," George prayed, "You know how much we want this baby. If You want us to have it, please let it be healthy. And if not, please give us Your strength and peace."

"It's a Girl"

When the time for the delivery came, Katie glanced at the mirror above her and noticed that it was turned away. At the moment of birth there were no cries, only stunned silence. The doctor broke that silence with the words George and Katie did not want to hear: "I'm sorry. It's a girl, but she is stillborn."

The Sandts were devastated. The next day George and his parents made funeral arrangements for baby Christine. Life had dealt them a crushing blow.

But it's in the crushing blows of life that we find God most tender toward us. The Sandts began to wonder if God would have them adopt a baby. They prayed about it and knew it was the right thing. In February 1969 a new little girl, just three months old, came into their lives. They named her Sandra, Sandy for short. She became the apple of their eye.

Three years later George and Katie discovered that Katie was pregnant again. Sandy was to have a little brother or sister. They couldn't contain their elation.

Months later, but still weeks before her due date, Katie went into labor. She was rushed to the hospital and she gave birth to a five-pound, six-ounce girl. While she was a preemie and had a good chance to live at that birth weight, there were other complications. The baby was placed in the intensive-care unit and remained critically ill for the next four days.

Doubly Devastated

Then the unthinkable happened, again. This tender little gift from heaven stopped breathing. For the second time, this godly family had lost a child. They were doubly devastated.

But the comfort of God more than equals the trauma of loss. He held them tightly to His divine chest, along with their little adopted girl, and gave them hope to go on. In fact, the Sandts decided if God didn't want them to have children by natural birth, they would adopt a second time.

A friend called Katie and told her she knew of a divorcee who was going to have a baby out of wedlock and wanted to place it in a good home. She already had a one-year-old boy named Tony; she didn't want another baby. Were the Sandts interested? Interested. They were ecstatic.

In February 1973 this young mother gave birth to a healthy girl, eight pounds, eight ounces. The Sandts drove to the hospital and named the little baby girl Brenda. After a year of not knowing for certain if the mother would actually give up her baby, a judge awarded Brenda to the Sandts as their legal, adopted daughter. They couldn't have been happier. God gave them two little girls, birthed by others but loved by them.

This is one of those prodigal stories that you wonder where the prodigal is. This all sounds like a "happily-ever-after" tale. What could possibly go wrong? Given enough time, almost anything.

Meet Your Biological Mother

Life was good for the Sandts. God blessed them. The girls both trusted Christ as Savior and were raised in a loving, Christian home.

They told their daughters that when the time was right, if they wanted to meet their biological mothers, the Sandts would help find them. Sandy showed little interest, for she was now an adult and happily married to Nathan. But Brenda, not quite 18, did want to locate her biological mother, and the Sandts were true to their word.

They traced her mother to Georgia and took Brenda to meet her. When she met her mother for the first time, she also met her biological brother, Tony, who was only one when she was born. He was now 19. Brenda and Tony bonded immediately. It was as if they were never apart. There was an immediate sense that they were brother and sister.

The Sandts invited Brenda's mother and Tony to their home in Pennsylvania to celebrate Brenda's 18th birthday. They came and everyone enjoyed having them there. After they returned to Georgia, dozens of phone calls between Brenda and Tony got them caught up on all their "missing" years.

Adopting a Brother

One night some time later, Brenda shocked her parents by asking, "Dad, Mom, would you consider adopting Tony as your son just as you adopted me?" They had never heard of adopting a 19-year old before but told Brenda they would consider it. They prayed much about it and decided it was the right thing to do. It would unite a brother and sister who had never known each other. So in July 1991 the Sandts adopted Tony as their adult son.

Meanwhile their oldest daughter, Sandy, and her husband, Nathan, and four-month-old grandson, Toby, were going through some traumatic changes in their life. Nathan was a small businessman in California and his business wasn't doing so well. In fact, they lost their business, their home, everything. They moved back home (literally, into an apartment in the walk-out basement of the Sandt home) in order to get back on their feet. This meant Dad and Mom, adopted sister and brother Brenda and Tony, were joined by Sandy, Nathan and Toby all under the same roof. This provided opportunity for Sandy and Brenda to be best friends again, and Tony and Nathan became best friends too. Nathan got a good job and life was on track again.

It's not when times are tough and life is hard that you have to watch out for Satan's attacks, but when life is good. The good times are the garden in which the seeds of prodigalism grow. That was true for the Sandt family.

Hints of Danger

Since there was instant rapport between all their kids, the family enjoyed their times together. Because Tony had just recently been saved, the Sandts used opportunities to help him grow spiritually. George and Tony enjoyed extended camping trips together for three consecutive years. Even though Tony had not lived with the Sandts during most of his life, the time he had spent with them now was precious.

Sandy and stepbrother Tony began to spend a great deal of time together—at times staying up late and watching a movie at home. But as Tony and Sandy spent more time together, communication between Tony and his adopted father and mother began to decrease. Tony just wouldn't say much.

Finally Tony decided to go to a college in Georgia. The Sandts thought this would be good for him, so George went with him to help find an apartment and get settled. If there was any concern over Tony becoming too close to Sandy, this would settle that. Over the next months, however, their son-in-law, Nathan, had to travel extensively for his job. Later the Sandts learned that when Nathan was away, Sandy would spend a great deal of time on the telephone talking with Tony in Georgia.

On one occasion when Nathan's boss sent him to Austria on an assignment, Sandy asked her mother to watch little Toby so she could go to Georgia and visit Tony. Her mother knew that wasn't a good idea, but Sandy was a married woman and did what she pleased.

The "What If" Questions

Two days after Nathan arrived home from Austria, Sandy arrived home from Georgia. Mothers and fathers have a sense when things aren't right, and both sensed things were not right between Sandy and Nathan. In fact, just days later Sandy announced that she was leaving Nathan and was going to drive to Georgia to be with Tony.

She went on to say that her marriage was a wreck and there was little hope for it. She took Toby and left for Georgia, never to return to Nathan.

Sleepless nights followed. Katie says there were the inevitable "what if" questions:

What if we had never adopted Tony, would this have happened?

What if Nathan and Sandy had stayed in California?

What if our two biological daughters had lived? Would our lives be in this mess?

There were plenty of questions, but no answers. God doesn't always provide answers. If He did, none of us would know the joy of relying totally on His strong and tender arms to bear us up during life's darkest hours.

As this godly father and mother cried out to God, they knew they had to do something more. They made trips to Georgia to see Sandy and try to talk her into coming home. But Tony and she lived in an apartment complex behind locked gates. Often they couldn't get to them. Neither Tony nor Sandy would accept their phone calls.

From Bad to Worse

As their relationships with Tony and Sandy deteriorated, the Sandts knew that Satan was working overtime. Once when they were away from home and Sandy knew they were gone, she drove up from Georgia and stole the title to the car the Sandts had loaned to Tony. She then forged George's signature on the back so they could sell the car.

On another occasion Sandy was to meet Nathan at the Charlotte airport to allow Toby to visit with his father. Sandy never showed. The trip was a bust.

Finally, Nathan decided that since his wife was living in adultery, and he had been betrayed by his best friend, he had to file for divorce. When the divorce papers were served on Sandy, she claimed she was her sister Brenda, and Nathan had to send pictures of her to the sheriff to prove they were serving the correct sister. Their marriage was over. Nathan was now a divorced father, but gained custody of their son. Sandy was a divorced mother, living with the man who, legally, although not biologically, was her brother. Unknown to George and Katie, Tony's birth mother began and finalized all necessary procedures to re-adopt Tony as her son.

Things seemed to be going from bad to worse. During this time Katie began to keep a journal—but not a journal of events in their troubled lives. It was a journal of verses on hope. She chronicled what the Bible had to say about hope. And what a blessing it was. It got a hurting mother through the darkest days of her life.

Life went on. As the years passed, Brenda met a young man and fell in love, and they decided to be married. They set a wedding date for the next March. Brenda asked for her father to give a parental blessing during the ceremony. The Sandts would gratefully give it but felt she needed to seek some reconciliation with her sister, Sandy, if Brenda's life was to be happy.

Prior to the wedding, Brenda wrote her older sister, whom she had not seen in years. It was a letter seeking forgiveness for her bitterness toward Sandy for what she had done. Sandy never responded. Later it was discovered that Sandy and Tony went to Hawaii and were married just two weeks before Brenda's wedding. And to add to the confusion, their ex-son-in-law Nathan had also met a fine Christian girl, and Kathryn and he were married just two weeks after Brenda's wedding. The Sandt's former son Tony has now become their son-in-law.

If you find yourself needing a playbill to identify all the actors and actresses in this family tragedy, join the club. When sin gets ahold of a heart, the damage is extensive and unbelievable.

Hope for the Troubled Heart

Some years have now passed since these heartbreaking events. Sandy's attitude toward her parents softened somewhat, but Tony was still angry at Mr. Sandt for attempting to interfere in the youthful wrong choices he made. It was only after Tony and Sandy moved to Virginia that George made a surprise visit to the store where Tony worked and asked if he could take him to lunch. Strangely, Tony agreed and the father and his adopted son talked. During their conversation the Lord met with them and God's love completely encircled them. A lot of issues were straightened out and they ended up hugging each other. That's a miracle in itself.

So have things returned to normal in the Sandt home? I'll let them speak for themselves. George says, "Define normal. There can never be a true normal in our home again. Our two adopted daughters have grown up in the Lord. Our oldest girl married and had our first grandson. Our adopted son fell in love with her. She left her husband to live with him. The two of them are now married and expecting their second child. Our youngest daughter has married and moved on with her life. They also have a child. Our first son-in-law, father of our first grandson, has now remarried, and they are expecting a child. We see them, but not as often as we would like. Normal? Define normal."

Things will never be as they used to be in the days of innocence. But prodigals do come back and things are getting better for the Sandts. Katie says, "God has worked many miracles. Tony and Sandy have now begun to come here for visits and we have gone to their house in Virginia. They had all of us down to their house for Christmas dinner. The week after Christmas we all went to Florida for a vacation week together. Sandy and Brenda are best friends again. Sandy and Tony have become involved in their church in Virginia. She recently asked for a recommendation for a devotional book for Tony and her to read together." Katie was clearly encouraged.

No, things never are the same when prodigalism is involved. But things can be better. When conviction of sin is real, and repentance is real, even prodigals go home again.

Are there yet problems to be reconciled? There certainly are. Nathan, Sandy's first husband, has yet to be reconciled with Tony, Sandy's present husband. The hurt is extremely deep and has not gone away.

Is there any hope? Katie says, "We know that will take another miracle—but look what God has done already!" God is in the miracle business.

EPILOGUE

Jesus was the Master Storyteller. He knew how to captivate an audience and hold their attention. His stories reflected the basic human emotions—love, hate, jealousy, pride, survival, etc. The parable of the prodigal son, the father and the older brother testifies to Jesus' ability to take these basic emotions and weave them into a spell-binding story.

But Jesus wasn't interested in spinning a yarn. He wanted to convey a truth. That's why He told parables: for the convicting truth they carried to their hearers.

Through this parable Jesus wants us to experience God's great love and concern for us. God is interested in every individual He created. He is interested in the proud prodigal, who has slapped his Creator in the face and says he has no need for God. He is interested in the self-righteous older brother, who has obeyed all the rules but is spiritually bankrupt. God is interested in all of us. He is interested in you.

The Master Storyteller ended His parable abruptly. Clearly Jesus wanted to convict the tax collectors and sinners of their self-willed distance from God and His Law. And just as clearly He wanted to convict the Pharisees and scribes of their self-righteous demands on God and His Law. But the artistic way the parable remains without a close leaves it open for continuing application. This is our parable as much as His.

There are still prodigals today. Maybe you're one of them. You belong to the family, but have forsaken your Father and His family. You've opted to live in the world of sin, despising the Father. But in the perfect timing of God, there's a famine coming. One day God will draw you back to the life of His family. When He does, go home. The Father's looking for you.

When you receive a prodigal back into church, there will be joy in heaven, but will there be joy in your heart? Maybe you haven't played the fool by wandering into the world, but have you been as self-righteous as the father's older son? Do you see yourself in Jesus' parable? Are you a stay-at-home prodigal? If so, join the celebration. Don't stay outside in the bitter cold. Come to the Father.

But most of this book has been about surviving the prodigals in your personal life—your children or your spouse. If your prodigal returns to you, will you be as compassionate as the father in Jesus' parable? Will you be eager to forgive? Or will you be just another older brother? The older brother in Jesus' story has many descendants.

It's difficult to admit we are wrong. Having announced we don't need God or His family, it's difficult to come crawling back. Being a prodigal is no fun. But even less fun is admitting we've been an older brother.

We're not told how the prodigal behaved after he came home again. And we're not told if the older brother abandoned his bitter pride and joined the celebration. We don't know what the brothers did after they hurt the father. But we do know what the father did.

Like our Heavenly Father, the father in Jesus' story loved each son—loved each individually, loved each unconditionally. Like our Heavenly Father, the father in Jesus' story made the first move toward reconciliation with both his sons. He made an overture toward each. This father knew how to survive the prodigals in his life.

You can survive, too, if you choose to treat your prodigals the way this father treated his. Here are some of the key words to survival: prayer; compassion; fairness; joy; forgiveness.

No one can make you a survivor, but you can be a survivor. Ask God to bring your prodigals home again. Scan the horizon for them. Anticipate their return. Do whatever you can to ease that return. Rejoice when they do return. And commit them daily to the Lord's tender care.

Whether your prodigal is of the runaway or stay-at-home variety, you can survive the prodigals in your life with God's help. Ask for His help. Never give up hope. Be a survivor.

Here's my prayer for all of you who are trying to survive the prodigals in your life:

Dear Father,

For every parent who is experiencing the pain of a prodigal, help them feel the strength of Your everlasting arms beneath them. For every husband or wife who has suffered from a prodigal spouse, draw them tightly to Your chest and cuddle them in Your love. For every church that suffers from prodigals and older brothers, raise up peacemakers to welcome prodigals home and help older brothers to do the same.

And when we're squeezed between the prodigals of our life, give us the tender compassion of the father. Make us more like him and less like his sons. When we are hurt by the prodigals in our lives, give us the grace of the father in Jesus' parable. Make us survivors, Father, by keeping hope alive.

Thank You, Lord, for the insights we have gleaned from Jesus' masterful parable. We who are grateful people pray in the name of our Savior.

Amen.

Do you have a prodigal story you'd like to share?
We'd love to hear from you.

Send your story to one of the following addresses.

E-mail: prodigals@backtothebible.org

Mail: Back to the Bible
Att. Publishing
P.O. Box 82808
Lincoln, NE 68501

Surviving the Prodigals in Your Life is also available on video!

If you are dealing with a prodigal in your life you need survival tactics, and author and Bible teacher Woodrow Kroll provides them—all from the soothing and calming setting of a beach in Bermuda.

With insight and compassion, *Surviving the Prodigals in Your Life* guides you in turning your hurt to hope—presenting an alternative to letting your feelings of disappointment and rejection drive your actions.

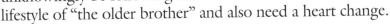

But there are potentially two prodigals in every story and Woodrow Kroll clearly shows how you may unknowingly be following the lifestyle of "the older brother" and also need a heart change.

Here are the keys to survival—whether your prodigal is of the runaway or stay-at-home variety. Here also is a call back to the Father if you find yourself far from home.

ISBN: 0-8474-1516-3

Call 1-800-759-2425 to order or visit your local Christian bookstore